S0-EGI-853

A STUDY GUIDE TO
Young Children in Action

Exercises in the Cognitively Oriented Preschool Curriculum

HIGH/SCOPE
EDUCATIONAL RESEARCH
FOUNDATION   Ypsilanti, Michigan

A STUDY GUIDE TO

Young Children
in Action

by **Mary Hohmann** with a foreword by David P. Weikart

THE
HIGH/SCOPE
PRESS

Published by
THE HIGH/SCOPE PRESS
High/Scope Educational Research Foundation
600 North River Street
Ypsilanti, Michigan 48197
(313) 485-2000

Copyright ©1983 by Mary Hohmann. All rights
reserved. No part of this work may be reproduced
or transmitted in any form or by any means, electronic or mechanical, including photocopying and
recording, or by any information storage or retrieval
system, without permission in writing from the
publisher.

Library of Congress Cataloging in Publication Data

Hohmann, Mary.
   A study guide to Young children in action.

   1. Education, Preschool—Handbooks, manuals,
etc. I. Hohmann, Mary. Young children in action.
II. Title.

LB1140.2.H588   1983   372′.21   83-13030

ISBN 0-931114-21-7

Printed in the United States of America

Contents

Foreword

Let's look at the basic issues

Before you begin the exercises presented in this study guide to **Young Children in Action,** we feel it is important to take a few minutes to look at some underlying issues in early childhood education. Typically, when you hear a statement like the one we have just made, you can sit back and relax, assured that a standard lecture will be forthcoming—a lecture outlining issues and presenting conclusions. You, as a student, may take a few notes for later reference and leave the lecture awed by the challenges in the early childhood education field. Such a beginning, however, would not set the proper tone for this study guide. Instead, we are going "to practice what we preach": active learning.

Experience is still the best teacher

People of all ages learn best through experience; that is, by constructing knowledge through their own actions. Young children learn about causality when, to their delight and continual amazement, they toss their feeding spoons (toys, food) from their highchairs and watch the objects fall to the floor with a crash. Caretakers are often dismayed and aggravated when children do such things, and they frequently lose patience unless they understand how this behavior relates to the way children's knowledge develops. Adolescents likewise test rules over and over again until, because of the natural consequences incurred, they find wisdom behind the rules; they too reach true understanding through experience. While as adults we are much better prepared to deal with abstract ideas, even we must work through a direct experience before true comprehension can occur.

To truly understand the High/Scope Cognitively Oriented Preschool Curriculum, you must put it into practice. Accordingly, this study guide is designed to give you practical experience. We present no pat answers. There are no easy solutions. You will construct your own learning with your colleagues, guided by the curriculum concepts. Let's get started now by trying some learning-through-experience activities.

Find a friend who has taught or is preparing to teach. Together, take a few minutes to list what you think the short- and long-term outcomes of early childhood education should be. Restrict your list to four or five. Don't read on until you have completed your list.

1.

2.

3.

4.

5.

When asked to do this, many people list such outcomes as (1) helping the child achieve his or her potential; (2) facilitating social adjustment with peers; (3) developing self-confidence; (4) developing motor skills; and (5) developing appreciation for the environment. How does this list compare with yours? Occasionally, someone will add "developing academic skills or academic readiness." Very rarely will someone list such practical, long-term outcomes as "preventing teenage pregnancy," "improving employment opportunities," or "reducing crime and delinquency." Did you list these areas?

Preschool education has long-term effects

Based on High/Scope research, we know something about the long-term effects of preschool that makes both individual and public commitment to early childhood education extremely important. For over 20 years we have been following two groups of disadvantaged children from age three to young adulthood. We have found that those persons with a preschool education, when compared with those who did not attend preschool, have

1. Better school achievement
2. Higher high school graduation and college attendance rates
3. Lower juvenile delinquency and adult crime rates
4. Less welfare dependency
5. Less teenage pregnancy and lower childbearing rates
6. Increased rates of job-holding and job-training

These practical outcomes have enormous social consequences for us as educators and for society at large.

Preschool programs must be of high quality

The research done by High/Scope and other institutions indicates that preschool programs "work." It is important to note, however, that they work only when they are of high quality. To be of high quality, preschool programs must exhibit the following characteristics:

- **An identifiable curriculum.** Research indicates that several theoretically diverse curricula are equally effective insofar as they have been studied to date, but that eclectic curricula (simple mixtures of ideas) are rarely effective.

- **Inservice training and supervision.** Once a curriculum has been chosen and a program is underway, ongoing inservice training and supervision is essential. Such training should be provided by a trained staff member who is skilled in implementing the curriculum and who will help the teaching staff apply the curriculum to individual children in the classroom.

- **Team teaching and planning.** Most teachers are more effective when they work in teams. A teaching team (like the one you will work with throughout this study guide) plans and develops joint strategies for working with children in the classroom. Team planning is most effective when it occurs each day.

- **Frequent evaluation.** Teaching staff need feedback on whether the program is working for the children in their classroom. Evaluation tells them what to emphasize and what program aspects may need further development. Effective evaluation can be done informally (for example, in the planning period when teaching staff look at each child's participation in the classroom) or much more formally (through outside assessment).

- **Parent involvement.** Parent involvement is an almost universal element of effective early childhood programs. Parents need to be involved not only in policy making but also in the educational process taking place in the classroom and at home.

- **Administrative and technical support and equipment.** Programs cannot operate in a chaotic environment; good staff management and basic support services are essential to allow the staff to focus on the difficult task of educating children.

There are real differences in approaches to learning

It is interesting to note that, when considering the general outcomes or goals for early childhood education, as we did in the first part of this Foreword, many persons fail to mention the cognitive processes that permit such general goals to be attained. Do you have an idea of

viii

what these processes might include? We would include the following as examples of what is important to us:

1. Solving problems
2. Assuming responsibility
3. Taking initiative
4. Being creative
5. Making plans

Let's try two exercises that will demonstrate the importance of cognitive processes in converting abstract goals into practice. The exercises are silly enough to remain with you as good mnemonic devices, yet are intended to make a serious point: there is a real difference between teaching approaches. Again, find a friend to do the exercises with you. Determine who will do the work and who will read the instructions and observe the work. Do not worry about who gets which role; after the first exercise, you will reverse roles. You will each need an 8½" x 11" piece of paper and a crayon or marker of some sort. If you are the observer, as you read the instructions to your partner pay special attention to the way in which your partner approaches the task, and how he or she responds to your instructions. You might jot down a few observations while the process is going on, so you can share them later.

The teacher-directed approach

The "observer" (teacher) should read these instructions aloud to the "worker" (child) and demonstrate each step.

1. Say: About one-fourth of the way from the top of your paper, draw a jagged line like this. (Demonstrate.)

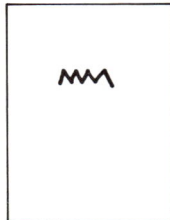

2. Say: Now draw two curved lines like this so they form the sides of a cup, almost meeting at the bottom. (Demonstrate.)

3. Say: Next, draw two parallel lines reaching to the bottom of the page, like this. (Demonstrate.)

4. Say: Now draw "ridges" on the cup, like this. (Demonstrate.)

5. Say: Now draw several more curved lines, starting at the bottom, like this. (Demonstrate.)

6. Say: Now that you have drawn your tulip, sign your name, put a date on the paper, and give it to me.

Take a few minutes to discuss how you both felt as you were doing this exercise. What did the observer see? How did the worker feel about the exercise? How did the observer feel about the exercise? How did the worker feel about the product? List some of these attitudes, feelings, and behaviors:

1.

2.

3.

4.

5.

The problem-solving approach

Now switch roles with your partner and do a second exercise. You will need the same size paper as the first exercise. Again, the person who is to be the observer can record observations, noting attitude and special behavior, while the worker carries out the task.

Say: Here's a problem for you to solve. Take a sheet of paper and make a paper airplane that glides. (Do not demonstrate.) Here are some paper airplanes that people often make (see illustrations below). But yours might not look like these.

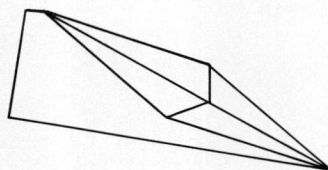

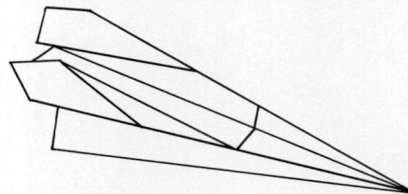

When the paper airplane is finished, take a few minutes with your partner to list what each of you felt while doing this exercise. What did the observer see? How did the worker feel about the exercise? How did the worker feel about the product? Did either of you try to fly the airplane? List some of these outcomes here:

1.

2.

3.

4.

5.

Now that you have done both the tulip and the airplane exercises, what differences do they represent in teaching and learning styles? Take a few minutes to list these differences:

1.

2.

3.

4.

5.

The teaching style we advocate

You have just experienced two different teaching styles and two different student roles. Based on these experiences, you should have a better vision of the teaching style we advocate to enhance children's problem-solving capabilities. Remember, *you* control your teaching style. We frequently find experienced teachers who are committed to children in a broad, humanistic way, but who employ the "tulip approach" of directed teaching rather than the "airplane approach" of problem solving, even though the tulip approach contrasts sharply with all their stated goals for children. If you are to be an effective teacher in a cognitively oriented preschool setting, you must allow children to work as problem solvers. Your teaching style must be consistent with this problem-solving approach to learning. We hope you will keep this advice firmly in mind as you work through this study guide.

Always remember that early childhood education affects the long-term outcomes of children's lives. As a preschool teacher, you play a critical role in helping children become effective adults in our society. Preschool programs are not effective if they are delivered in an offhand and uninformed manner. The key to high quality program delivery is *you*, the teacher. Children's futures are significantly related to your ability to deliver such programs of high quality as the High/Scope Cognitively Oriented Preschool Curriculum. Both the opportunity and the responsibility are clearly yours.

David P. Weikart
President
High/Scope Educational Research Foundation
August 1983

About this book

This study guide is for students and practitioners of the High/Scope Cognitively Oriented Preschool Curriculum. The exercises are designed for people who are willing to immerse themselves totally in an approach to preschool learning that provides the elements needed to establish a high quality early childhood education program.

Exercises in this study guide are participatory, calling for you to learn by doing. The exercises "teach" you the same way the High/Scope curriculum "teaches children"—by providing active-learning experiences. Few answers can be found simply by turning to the appropriate page in the accompanying manual, **Young Children in Action.** A knowledge of the manual is expected, however, and together with your own experience and observations, this knowledge should guide you to answers and solutions.

For some of the exercises in each chapter, you will need access to a preschool classroom where you can observe and interact with teaching staff and children. This will help you realize that the best theories often fall apart in the face of everyday realities, and realities are what teaching staff must learn to deal with effectively.

From time to time you will need a preschool-aged child you can work with as you do the exercises in this book. For your "child study," you might choose someone in the preschool class you are observing, or you might choose a young neighbor, sibling, cousin, niece, or nephew. Perhaps you will find a child through volunteer work in a local day care center, YMCA class, Sunday school, or music class. Your work with this child will be vital to your understanding of young children, so the sooner you become acquainted, the better. (More details about the "child-study" child are given in Chapter 5 on page 80.)

You will need to choose a teaching team. Since the Cognitively Oriented Preschool Curriculum is based on a team approach to problem solving, many of the exercises in this book are designed to be done with a team, in much the same way that teaching and planning are done in a preschool classroom. Although you won't need to identify your teaching team until Chapter 3, you should start thinking now about people you might work with effectively.

There is no answer book accompanying this study guide, just as there is no answer book for teaching staff as they confront the everyday issues of early childhood education in their preschool classrooms and day care centers. When an answer or solution does not work, your child and teaching team will help you design and implement alternatives.

The exercises in this book are meant to be enjoyed in the same way that we hope you enjoy working with young children. We hope these exercises, like active learning and teamwork, will be both challenging and satisfying.

1/ Arranging & equipping the classroom

The arrangement of a cognitively oriented classroom reflects the belief that children learn best in a stimulating but ordered environment in which they can make choices and act on them. The classroom is divided into well-defined work areas, and the materials in each area are logically organized and clearly labeled, which enables the children to act independently and with as much control over the classroom environment as possible.

1. Room arrangement effectiveness

Room arrangement affects the way both children and adults feel about themselves and interact with others.

a) Describe how you, as a child, dealt with the task of cleaning your room. What made this chore difficult? Easy?

b) Your uncle has died and left his entire estate to you. You are selling his house, which includes an extensive and valuable machine shop. You have a buyer who is particularly interested in the machine shop which, unfortunately, is in great disarray. In order to present the machine shop in the most marketable light, you have to organize it even though you don't know a socket wrench from a drill press. Describe the steps you would go through to accomplish this task.

1

c) Review room arrangement checklist items 1-28 in **Young Children in Action,** pages 294-98. Describe how children and adults would behave and feel in a classroom where all of these criteria are met.

2. Promoting key experiences through room arrangement

Room arrangement sets the stage for many of the key experiences. For example, by organizing the room into several well-defined work areas where materials are easily accessible, adults are enabling children to "choose materials, activities, and purposes," a key experience in active learning. Turn to the list of key experiences on pages 3-6 in **Young Children in Action.** In the chart below, list ten more key experiences that are directly promoted by a well-organized classroom, and briefly note how.

Topic	Key Experience	How Room Arrangement Promotes Key Experiences
active learning	choosing materials, activities, purposes	A room that is organized for children so that they can readily find things enables them to see what is available and to choose and get materials for themselves.

3. Floor plans

Use the checklist below (taken from **Young Children in Action,** pp. 294-5) to complete the following exercises:

a) Evaluate the three room arrangement floor plans (classrooms A, B, and C) presented on pages 5-7.

b) Draw and label a rearrangement of each room in the space provided, so that all the elements in the checklist are included.

_____**Room Arrangement Checklist**_____

Classroom

A B C
☐ ☐ ☐   1. The room is divided into several distinct areas or interest centers (house, art, block, quiet, construction, sand and water, music and movement, animal and plant).

A B C
☐ ☐ ☐   2. Boundaries are well defined by low shelves, stable screens, or walls with openings, so that children and adults can see into areas.

A B C
☐ ☐ ☐   3. Each area has an adequate amount of space for children and their use of materials.

A B C
☐ ☐ ☐   4. Tables are incorporated into the work areas.

A B C
☐ ☐ ☐   5. The art area is near the sink.

A B C
☐ ☐ ☐   6. Work areas are not cluttered with unnecessary furniture or materials.

A B C
☐ ☐ ☐   7. The areas are in corners or on the edges of the room and open into a central planning or meeting area.

Classroom

A B C
☐ ☐ ☐   8. The art area floor is tiled.

A B C
☐ ☐ ☐   9. The block area floor is carpeted.

A B C
☐ ☐ ☐   10. Traffic flow permits children to work without interruption.

A B C
☐ ☐ ☐   11. The house and block areas are near each other for interrelated play.

A B C
☐ ☐ ☐   12. The noisier areas are not close to the quieter areas.

A B C
☐ ☐ ☐   13. Individual storage space (dishtubs, empty gallon containers, boxes, baskets) and coat space are provided for each child to store his or her personal belongings. These storage spaces are labeled and placed low enough so that children can use them independently.

A B C
☐ ☐ ☐   14. Riding toys, a workbench, a sand table, table and chairs, are _not_ included in the block area.

4

An Indoor-Outdoor, Warm-Climate Classroom

Classroom A

Low Fence

Low Fence

Outdoor Court

Table

Sand

Outdoor Sink

Quiet Area

House Area

Garden

Door to Outside Court

Shelf

Shelf

Table

Easels

Block Area

Art Area

Coat Hooks

Individual Storage Tubs

Shelf

Sink

Door to Hallway

Tiled Floor

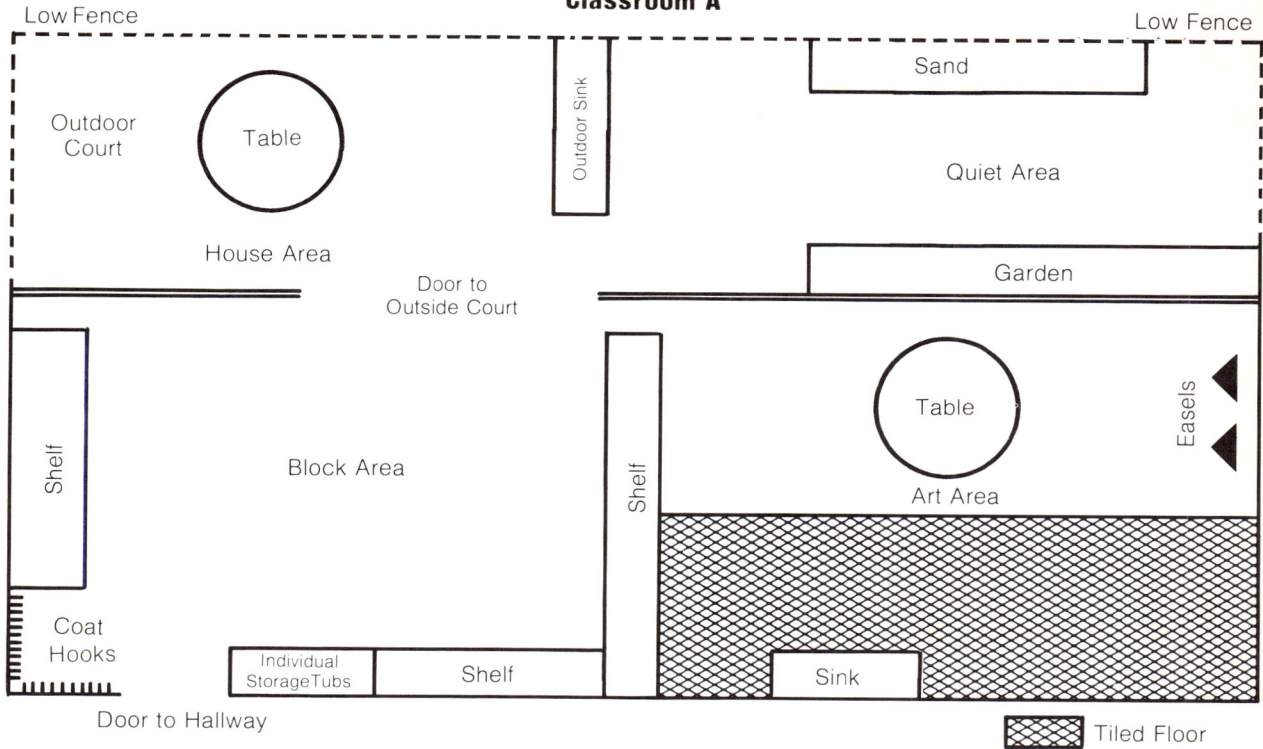

Rearranged Classroom A

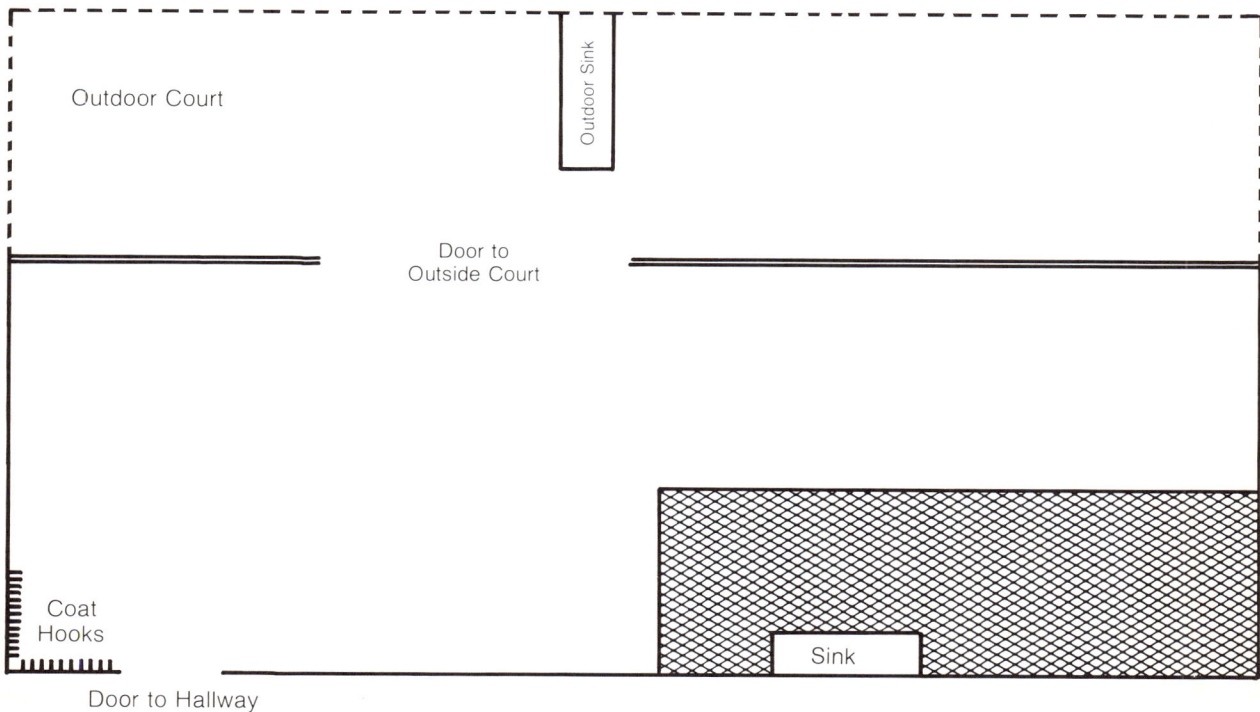

Outdoor Court

Outdoor Sink

Door to Outside Court

Coat Hooks

Sink

Door to Hallway

5

Classroom B

Block Area

Table

Shelf

Musical Instruments & Books

Shelf

Table

House Area

Shelf

Teacher Desk

Shelf

Table

Shelf

Table

Workbench

Art/Quiet Area

Shelf

Individual Storage Tubs

Coat Rack

Sink

Easels

Door

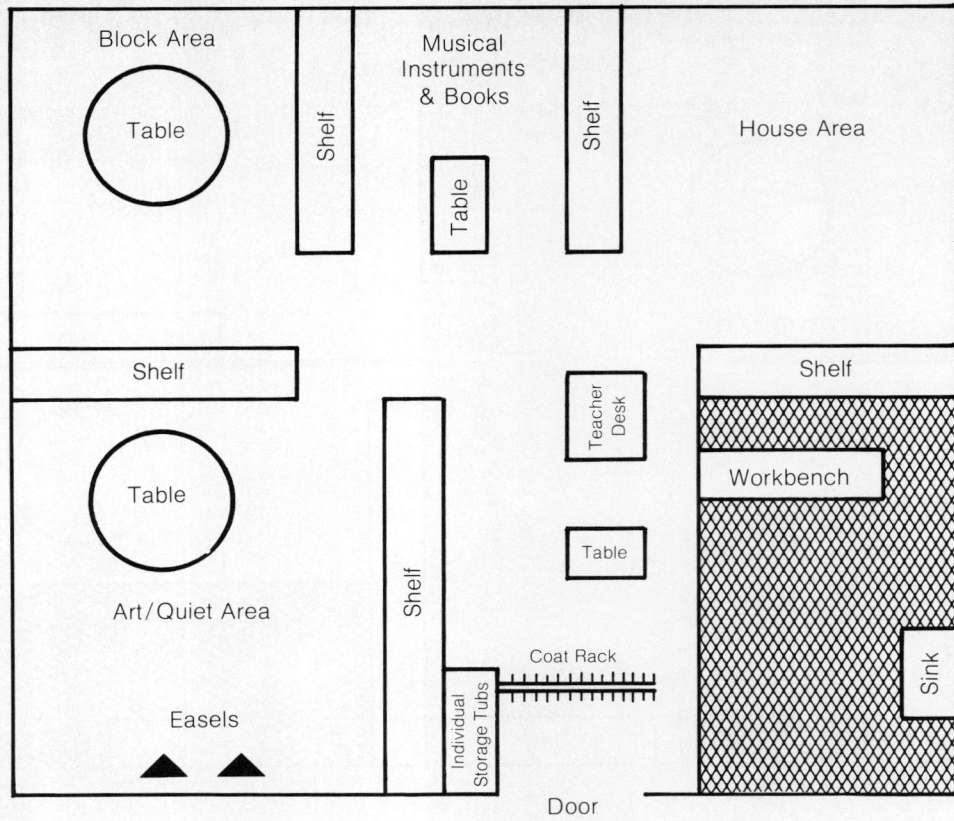

Rearranged Classroom B

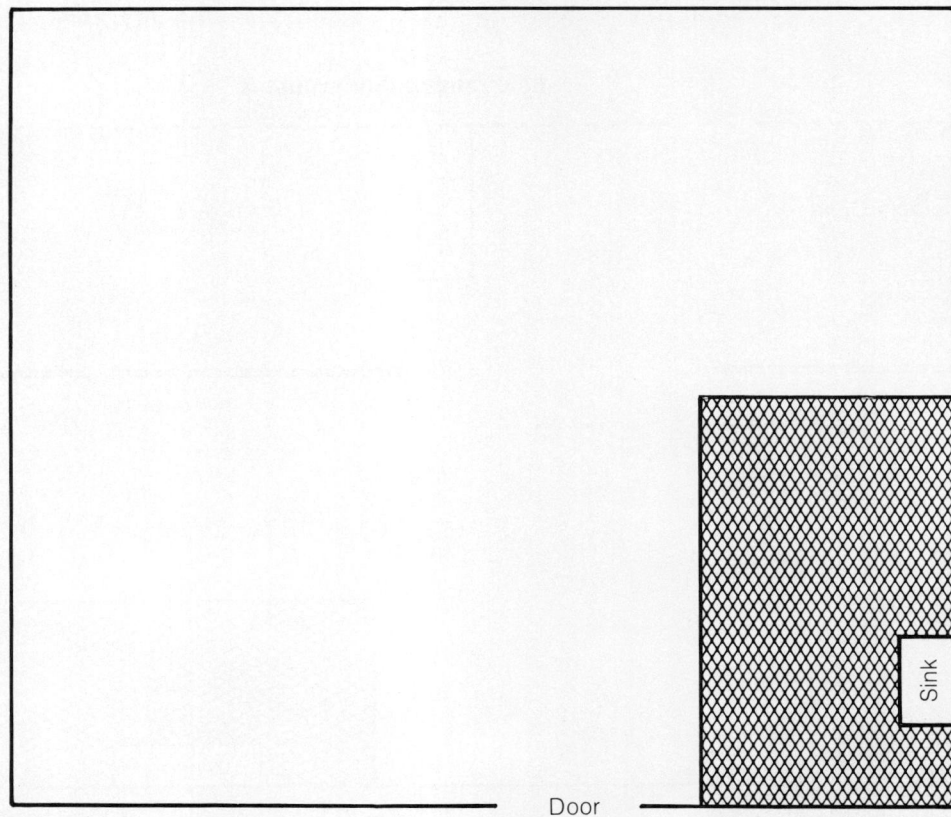

Sink

Door

Classroom C

Construction Area

Closet

Easel

Sink

Music Area

Table

Bathroom

Workbench

Back Door

House Area

Shelf

Quiet Area

Table

Shelf

Block Area

Coat Rack

Shelf

Shelf

Storage Tubs

Storage Tubs

Shelf

Art Area

Front Door

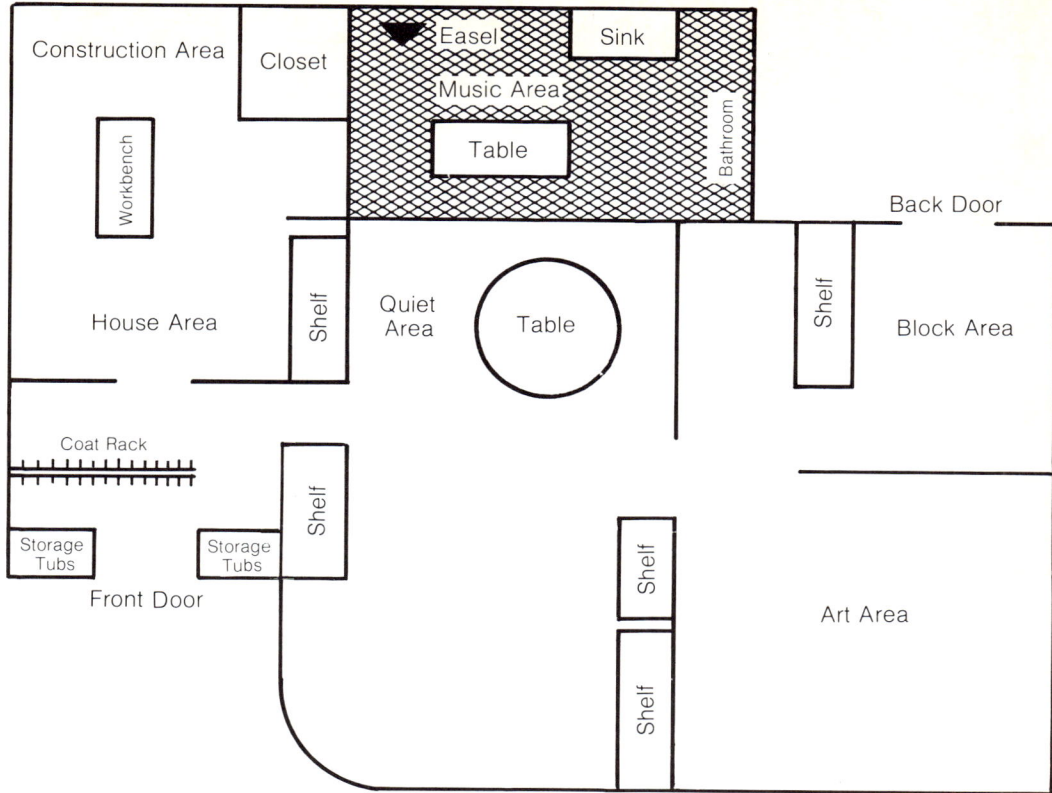

Rearranged Classroom C

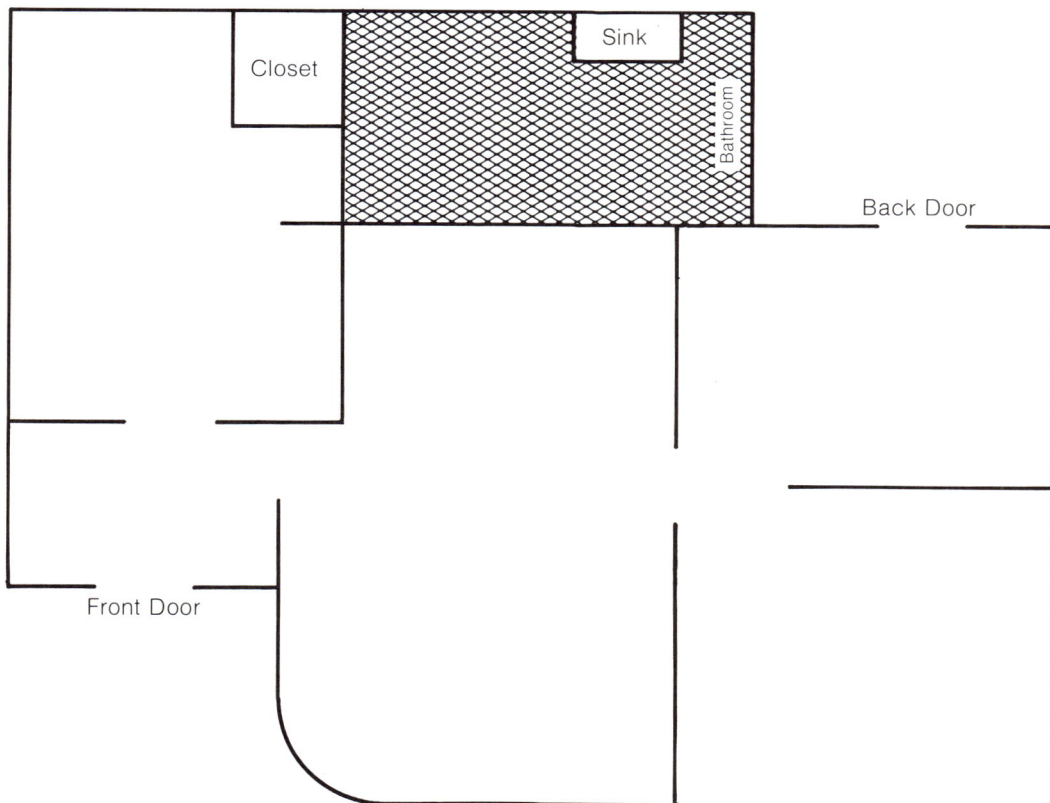

Closet

Sink

Bathroom

Back Door

Front Door

7

4. Work areas and materials

Examine the pictures of classrooms E, F, and G on the facing page and then complete these exercises:

a) Write in the name of the work area represented in each picture.

b) Evaluate each work area, using as a guide checklist items 15-27 below (taken from **Young Children in Action,** pp. 295-96).

c) List the changes you think are necessary to bring each work area in line with the checklist.

_____**Room Arrangement Checklist (continued)**_____

Classroom

E F G
☐ ☐ ☐ 15. Materials are stored in the area where they are used.

E F G
☐ ☐ ☐ 16. Shelves, drawers, and containers are labeled with a sample object or with pictures, photographs, or outlines of the contents.

E F G
☐ ☐ ☐ 17. Identical and similar items are stored together.

E F G
☐ ☐ ☐ 18. Sets of materials in different sizes are hung or stored so that size differences are apparent.

E F G
☐ ☐ ☐ 19. Materials within each area are easily accessible to children.

E F G
☐ ☐ ☐ 20. All materials within children's sight and reach can be used by children.

E F G
☐ ☐ ☐ 21. There is an adequate amount and variety of materials in each area.

E F G
☐ ☐ ☐ 22. Each area contains unstructured materials that can be used in many ways. Example: poker chips can be used for counting, stacking, matching, sorting, representing food or money.

Classroom

E F G
☐ ☐ ☐ 23. There is a variety of materials available to children for achieving their goals. Examples: papers can be put together with glue, paste, tape, staples, paper clips, string, rubber bands; a house can be made with blocks, paper, wood at workbench, playdough, paint.

E F G
☐ ☐ ☐ 24. There are enough materials in each area for children to work simultaneously.

E F G
☐ ☐ ☐ 25. There are materials that can be manipulated and actively explored in each area.

E F G
☐ ☐ ☐ 26. There are materials that can be used for pretending or making representations in each area.

E F G
☐ ☐ ☐ 27. There are many real things (plants, animals, utensils, tools, and instruments) that children can explore in each area.

Classroom E: The _____ Area   Changes

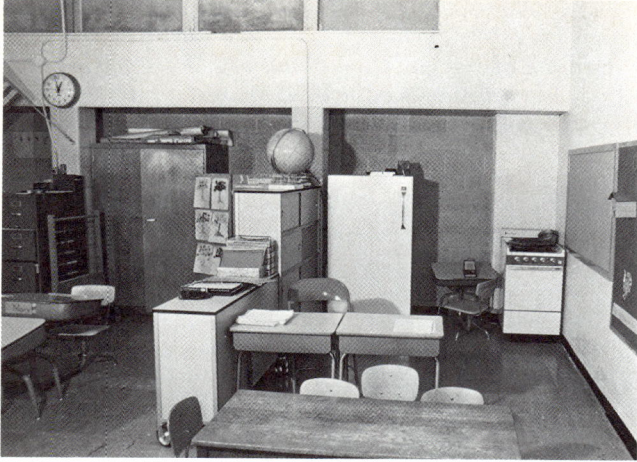

Classroom F: The _____ Area   Changes

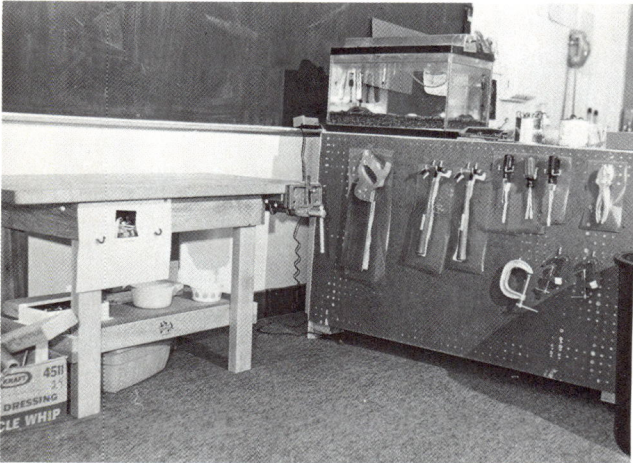

Classroom G: The _____ Area   Changes

5. Designing and equipping your own preschool classroom

As a community-service project your apartment building/dorm/sorority/fraternity/co-op/business/neighborhood/family is starting a preschool center, or classroom, for 15 three- and four-year-old children. Because of your interest in early childhood education, you have been asked to take charge of arranging and equipping the room(s) that will serve as the preschool classroom.

a) Select the room(s) in your current apartment/dorm/sorority/fraternity/co-op/business/house that is(are) most suited to become a preschool classroom.

b) Make a floor-plan sketch of the room(s) you have selected.

c) Decide which work areas you will include in the classroom and locate them on your floor plan according to the principles in checklist items 1-14 presented earlier.

_____**Your Floor Plan**_____

d) You have a budget of $500 for classroom materials. Use as a guide an actual catalog of preschool supplies or the list of materials and prices provided below. Decide what materials you will include in each work area and fill out the following chart.

Commercial Materials	Found/Donated Materials
_____ Area	
_____ Area	
_____ Area	
_____ Area	
_____ Area	

Commerical Materials Price List

$ 1.50	bells
12.95	cardboard blocks
16.50	child-sized chairs
84.00	child-sized toy refrigerator
84.00	child-sized toy sink
84.00	child-sized toy stove
7.07/5 lb	clay
.80/pkg	construction paper
13.80/doz	crayons
17.95	dishes
10.50	drum
44.95	easel
9.69/gal	glue
136.50	kidney-shaped tables
5.95	lacing boards
9.40	Lincoln Logs
26.00	Loc Blocks
1.95/ea	magnet
2.29/set	markers
40.00	mirror
6.95/doz	paint brushes
2.07/pt	paste
12.95	pegboard
1.75	plastic storage containers
2.50/ea	playdough
11.95	pots and pans
24.00/set of 12	powder paint
5.75/ea	puppets
100.00	record player
1.80	sandblocks
143.50	sand table
1.60/roll	transparent tape
150.00	shelves
15.30	stapler
1.18/box	staples
4.20	tambourine
15.30	tape recorder
2.95	telephone
6.95	toy farm animals
2.10	triangle
87.95/set of 32	wooden unit blocks
146.95/set of 55	wooden unit blocks

Found Materials

books	jewelry
bottle caps	measuring cups
broom	packing materials
buttons	pans
cardboard	popsicle sticks
carpet squares	silverware
clothes	sponges
dishes	spools
dolls	tricycles
dustpan	tubes
empty cartons	wagon
foam	wallpaper
hats	wood scraps

e) Evaluate your materials list according to the checklist for each work area you've selected. (These checklists can be found in **Young Children in Action,** pp. 296-97.) Make any changes necessary.

11

f) Your budget has just been slashed. You can spend only $200 on commercial materials, but you have been offered unlimited help in making and collecting found materials. Revise your chart, eliminating some commercial materials and showing what additional materials you will make or find so you still meet the checklist criteria for each area.

Commercial Materials	Found/Donated Materials	Commercial Materials Price List	
Area		$ 1.50	bells
		12.95	cardboard blocks
		16.50	child-sized chairs
		84.00	child-sized toy refrigerator
		84.00	child-sized toy sink
		84.00	child-sized toy stove
		7.07/5 lb	clay
Area		.80/pkg	construction paper
		13.80/doz	crayons
		17.95	dishes
		10.50	drum
		44.95	easel
		9.69/gal	glue
		136.50	kidney-shaped tables
		5.95	lacing boards
Area		9.40	Lincoln Logs
		26.00	Loc Blocks
		1.95/ea	magnet
		2.29/set	markers
		40.00	mirror
		6.95/doz	paint brushes
		2.07/pt	paste
		12.95	pegboard
Area		1.75	plastic storage containers
		2.50/ea	playdough
		11.95	pots and pans
		24.00/set of 12	powder paint
		5.75/ea	puppets
		100.00	record player
		1.80	sandblocks
		143.50	sand table
Area		1.60/roll	transparent tape
		150.00	shelves
		15.30	stapler
		1.18/box	staples
		4.20	tambourine
		15.30	tape recorder
		2.95	telephone
		6.95	toy farm animals
		2.10	triangle
		87.95/set of 32	wooden unit blocks
		146.95/set of 55	wooden unit blocks

Found Materials

books	jewelry
bottle caps	measuring cups
broom	packing materials
buttons	pans
cardboard	popsicle sticks
carpet squares	silverware
clothes	sponges
dishes	spools
dolls	tricycles
dustpan	tubes
empty cartons	wagon
foam	wallpaper
hats	wood scraps

6. Setting up your own outdoor play space

Outdoor play space is as important as indoor play space. To plan the outdoor play space for your preschool center, review pages 51-52 in **Young Children in Action.**

a) Select an outdoor space near your current apartment/dorm/sorority/fraternity/co-op/business/house. Below, draw a plan to turn the space you have selected into an outdoor play space. Include boundaries, major features, and pieces of equipment.

_____**Your Outdoor Play Space**_____

b) Evaluate your outdoor play space according to the following questions taken from the filmstrip *Where Can Children Play: Planning Play Spaces for Young Children*[1] by Steen B. Esbensen:

1. How far is the play space from the entrance to the classroom?

2. Do the children have to cross a road to get to the play space?

3. How is the play space enclosed?

4. Are the play areas clearly identifiable?

5. Is there an area with bushes, shrubs, and other landscaping features for quiet retreat?

6. Is there a mound or hill to climb on or to slide down in the winter?

7. Is water accessible to the sand play area?

8. Have you provided space for social and dramatic play?

9. Is there an area that enables the children to stretch, pull, balance, and generally develop their large motor skills?

10. Is there a flat, open space for ball games?

11. Is shade provided?

12. Are there any obstacles to supervision created by the arrangement of the equipment and landscaping features of the site?

13. Is the sand area enclosed and landscaped to prevent sand loss?

14. Is there a flat work surface (such as a table top) in the sand area?

15. Are a variety of textures used? Examples: sand, grass, rocks, tree stumps, other natural landscaping features.

16. Does the slide stop in the only sand area on the site?

7. Labeling classroom materials

Labeling refers to the process of marking where materials go. Labels made from objects, tracings, catalog pictures, or photographs of materials help children locate and return classroom materials.

a) As children match objects to labels, they are classifying, seriating, or noting spatial relations. (See the listing of key experiences on pages 3-6 of **Young Children in Action**.) Look at the photographs from **Young Children in Action** listed below. Briefly describe or draw the labels shown and decide whether the labels are promoting classifying, seriating, and/or noting spatial relations.

Photograph	Description	What Labels Promote
p. 38		

---

[1]Used with permission of the author. See page 18 for complete reference.

14

Photograph	Description	What Labels Promote
p. 41		
p. 174		
p. 219		

b) Select one of the materials you bought in exercise 5d. Draw or describe how you would label it and indicate what the label promotes.

c) Look at the photograph on page 261 in **Young Children in Action.** Why is it important to include children in the labeling process?

15

8. Observing a classroom

Visit a preschool classroom. Study carefully how it is arranged and equipped. Look for the items on the checklist in **Young Children in Action,** pages 294-98, and check off the items you find.

a) What are this classroom's strengths regarding room arrangement?

b) If this were your classroom, what room arrangement or equipment changes would you make to meet more of the checklist criteria?

9. Room arrangement issues to ponder

a) Often when an individual is working on a project, her or his work space is a mess for days at a time. Why does this work for an individual but not for groups of preschoolers?

b) Some adults think an organized room arrangement interferes with children's spontaneity. What do you think and why?

c) In the middle of the school year, due to circumstances beyond your control, you must move your preschool from one church basement to another. How would you prepare children for the move and include them in the moving process?

d) Turn back to exercise 5. What room arrangement modifications would you make for a visually impaired child? Hearing impaired child? Physically impaired child? Mentally impaired child?

10. Room arrangement projects

a) Visit as many preschool classrooms as you can. Evaluate them using the room arrangement checklist in **Young Children in Action,** pages 294-98. Photograph or sketch each classroom. The resulting room arrangement album will serve you well when you set up your own classroom.

b) Work with a teaching team to help set up an actual preschool classroom. Document room arrangement changes and children's responses as changes occur over the year.

c) Make up, try out, evaluate, and modify games that acquaint children with room arrangement, names of work areas, and locations of materials.

d) Ask several children to represent their preschool classrooms in two or three dimensions. Collect or photograph these representations.

Films and Publications

Films

Arranging the Classroom: Case Study of the High/Scope Preschool [PS190]
Color filmstrip and cassette tape; 15 min
A teacher from the High/Scope Preschool describes her attempts to implement principles of room arrangement and to select and organize materials to promote intellectual development—that is, to give children opportunities to exercise emerging cognitive abilities that are critical to the formation of more mature modes of thinking. She discusses the changes in her classroom structure and equipment over the course of a year.

The Block Area
[PS191] *Set of five color filmstrips and cassette tapes; 38.7 min total*
For preschool teachers who wish to establish interest areas in their classrooms. The focus is on the block area but the information is applicable to interest areas in general and to the teacher's role as a resource and guide for active learning.

1. Setting Up a Block Area *(7.5 min)*
How to set up a block area and arrange it so that it is well placed and logically organized; how to equip the area initially and then add materials as the children become more familiar with the area.

2. A Place to Explore New Materials *(6.5 min)*
How children explore materials by trying things out, using their senses, arranging objects, etc., and what a teacher can do to facilitate children's explorations.

3. A Place to Build All Kinds of Structures *(9 min)*
How children build up, out, around—shows examples of typical structures and suggests strategies a teacher can use to encourage purposeful building.

4. A Place to Represent Things *(8.7 min)*
Structures children build in the block area—roads, sidewalks, barns, garages, houses—and ways a teacher can respond to and support this important work of young children.

5. Observing a Child in the Block Area *(7 min)*
Lynnette builds a large structure in the block area and a teacher observes and works with her. The narrator discusses the kinds of questions a teacher might ask in this situation and the strategies she could use to help Lynnette extend and represent her structure.

Helping Children Make Choices and Decisions
[PS100] *Set of five 16mm films; color, sound; 33 min total*
Five short films that deal with aspects of the teacher's role in helping children make responsible, thoughtful, creative choices. The films were produced in several Head Start centers. Some of the dialogue is in Spanish.

1. A Good Classroom Is a Classroom Full of Choices
[PS101] *(7 min)*
Children should be able to choose what they're going to do, where they're going to work, what materials they'll use, who they'll work with. This film shows how teachers can structure the classroom environment and the children's activities to provide opportunities to make and carry out such critical choices.

Where Can Children Play
[PS120] *Set of three color filmstrips and cassettes; 35 min total*
The three presentations contained in this package are designed to provide an understanding of the problem of space for children in housing developments, playgrounds, and play areas in schools and parks.

The package set is intended to provide the users with audio-visual material for three workshop sessions during which they can proceed from a general understanding of the problem to a precise design framework for developing appropriate play opportunities on their site.

Print scripts and a discussion guide are included.

Where Can Children Play: An International Overview
[PS121] *(16 min)*
Summarizes the findings of an international study of public policies on space for children's play activities and suggests some considerations for qualitative development of a residential site when space standards exist.

Planning Play Spaces for Young Children
[PS122] *(10 min)*
Provides a design framework for the development of a particular play space. Some guidelines for the development of appropriate play environments for children under six years of age are suggested.

Planning Play Spaces for School-Age Children
[PS123] *(9 min)*
Surveys the play activities commonly preferred by six- to fourteen-year-olds and presents some design considerations for providing such child-responsive environments.

Publications

Room Arrangement and Materials
(#3 Elementary Series)
Author: S. Mainwaring; booklet (44 pages); 1977
The book gives details for setting up an environment in which children can test and express their ideas, make decisions, solve problems, apply their own reasoning to diverse situations, and share their experiences with others. This booklet describes the kinds of planning that the teaching staff could use to produce this learning environment. Strategies are provided for setting up interest areas, changing and developing an area, and keeping interest areas challenging. An extensive appendix lists equipment, supplies, and resources for 15 interest areas.

Write or call the High/Scope Foundation, 600 North River Street, Ypsilanti, MI 48197, (313) 485-2000 to obtain information on ordering these materials.

2/Establishing a daily routine

A consistent daily routine is a framework. It frees children and adults from worrying about or having to decide what comes next, and it enables them to use their creative energies on the tasks at hand. A daily routine is designed to accomplish three major goals:

- *Provide children with a plan-do-review process to help them explore, design, and carry out projects and make decisions.*

- *Provide for many types of interaction—small and large group, adult to child, child to child, and adult teamwork—and for times when activities are child-initiated or adult-initiated.*

- *Provide children with enough time to work in a variety of environments— inside, outside, on field trips, in various work areas.*

When the daily routine is well implemented it can provide a multifaceted structure in which children and adults can be active and creative.

1. Why a daily routine?

In the view of **Young Children in Action** (p. 58), "A consistent routine is a framework. It frees children and adults alike from worrying about or having to decide what comes next and enables them to use their creative energies on the tasks at hand." Not everyone agrees with this view, however. Some people feel that a consistent daily routine constrains and curbs creative energies. A child just gets started on a building, for example, but has to stop, not because he or she has completed building a structure but simply because it is clean-up time. Keeping these views in mind, complete the following exercises as if you were addressing a group of preschool parents:

a) List the *pros* of a consistent daily routine. How does it assist children? How does it assist adults?

b) List the *cons* of a consistent daily routine.

c) How does a consistent daily routine affect children's feelings of security, independence, and control over their environment?

d) If you were in charge of a preschool classroom would you have a consistent daily routine? Why or why not?

2. Blocks of time within a daily routine

A daily routine is made up of a sequence of time blocks. Each time block has a name so that children and adults can easily refer to it and talk about what happens during that time. Below, list the time blocks within a daily routine as outlined in **Young Children in Action,** pages 59-60, and identify the characteristics of each time block.

Name of Time Block	Characteristics

3. Sequencing the daily routine

The overall sequence of a daily routine depends on what works best for each classroom. For example, in some centers a meal time must be included in the schedule while in others it is not. In some centers the climate often determines when and if an outdoor time occurs. "The particular arrangement is not important as long as each element is included. However *planning time, work time, clean-up time,* and *recall* should always follow one right after another, and *work time* should be the longest single time period." (**Young Children in Action,** p. 60)

Philip and Elaine are two teachers in the Scoville Junction Preschool. Use the following descriptions of elements of their daily routine to complete exercises *a-d.*

a) Identify the time of day described in each case.

Time of Day_____

It is a bright autumn day. The children all go outside where they climb, swing, slide, play in the sand, play ball, and ride the wheel toys. Elaine is helping children hang by their knees from the climber while Philip is helping some children set up an obstacle course.

Time of Day_____

Several children in the art area are making collages out of styrofoam bits, scraps of fabric, newsprint, wood scraps, foil, and paper. They call Philip over because they can't get the foil to stick. He helps them find and try out alternatives to glue. Elaine has helped a group of children find space to build a variety of block structures and is now in the house area where she knocks on the door of what appears to be a doctor's office.
"What's wrong today?" a "doctor" greets her.
"My arm hurts. Can you help me?" she asks.
"Sure, come on in."
In the music area, two children are playing tambourines and making up a dance, while in the quiet area a group of children play store, using dominoes, rig-a-jigs, and puzzle pieces as props.

Time of Day_____

In the art area, Philip and half of the children in the classroom are working with playdough, toothpicks, and pipe cleaners. Some children are making people, others are making cakes, and others are just rolling, flattening, and squeezing the playdough. In the quiet area, Elaine and the rest of the children are finding things with holes and stringing them in various patterns.

Time of Day_____

"What would you like to do today?" Elaine and Philip ask each child. Some children respond by pointing to an area. Others get a toy they'd like to use. Others describe what they'll be doing while Philip or Elaine write down their plans and then read back their words.

Time of Day_____

Elaine puts on a record and asks all the children to decide which parts of their bodies they could move to the music. "Let's start with Carole," Philip suggests. "Carole can give her idea and then, since Paul is next to Carole, Paul can tell us his idea next, and we'll go around until everyone has had a chance to tell us how to move."

Time of Day_____

While the children have juice and carrot sticks, Philip and Elaine ask each one to show or tell about what they did that day. They ask questions about individual activities and suggest ways each child might continue the activity the next day. They also encourage the children to listen attentively to each speaker.

Time of Day_____

The art area is littered with containers of glue and collage scraps. Philip helps the collage makers decide who is going to collect the glue bottles, who is going to gather up the wood scraps, and so on. The block builders are busy piling each other up with blocks and returning them to the shelf. The music makers have joined the store people in the quiet area where everyone is sorting and replacing puzzle pieces, dominoes, and rig-a-jigs. Elaine is helping the "doctors" dismantle their office and return the house area to normal.

b) How would you sequence the blocks of time of Philip and Elaine's daily routine?

   1.

   2.

   3.

   4.

   5.

   6.

   7.

c) Why did you sequence the routine as you did?

d) How would you change the sequence if it were winter and the children had to put on boots, caps, mittens, and coats for outside time?

4. A daily routine for your center

In Chapter 1, exercise 5, you arranged and equipped a preschool classroom. Your next task is to establish a routine for the 15 children who are in the classroom.

The following children attend your preschool. They will appear in exercises throughout the rest of this book. If you want to change the names of any of these children to names of similar children you know, change them on this list and throughout the exercises in this book.

Sasha	3½ years	has Down's Syndrome
Denise	3 years	shy, nonverbal
Timmy	4½ years	outgoing, lots to say
Raymond	4 years	very active
Elise	4½ years	energetic
Mike, Sam	3 years	twins
Michelle	4½ years	has been in another preschool
Clarice	3 years	prone to tantrums
Corey	3½ years	quiet, often plays alone
Brenda	4½ years	always has something to say
Jamison	4 years	Brenda's cousin
Marketta	3 years	very quiet, cries often
Troy	3 years	has difficulty getting along with other children
Lynnette	4½ years	full of energy and ideas
Juanita	4 years	joins class later, Spanish-speaking, see Chapter 6

a) Make up a daily routine for your preschool program which runs from 2:00 to 4:30 p.m.

Time Interval	Name of Time Block

b) Give a rationale for the sequence of your routine.

c) What would you do with children who didn't get picked up promptly at 4:30 p.m.?

5. Helping children learn the daily routine

For a daily routine to be effective, adults and children alike need to know the names of the time blocks and their sequence. For adults this is a relatively easy task. Preschool children, however, need time and help. Review the suggestions for helping children learn the daily routine in **Young Children in Action,** pages 58-61, and then answer the following questions:

a) Which of these suggestions would you use in your preschool classroom? Why?

b) You have a Down's Syndrome child, Sasha, in your classroom. How would you help Sasha learn the daily routine?

6. Planning time

The following exercises describe some planning-time situations you might encounter in your preschool classroom. For assistance in dealing with them, you can refer to pages 61-72 in **Young Children in Action.**

a) You and a co-teacher have been running your preschool classroom for a month now and most of the children understand planning time. This is Denise's first day, however. She has just turned three and appears to be quite shy. All the rest of the children have made and begun their plans. When you ask Denise what she would like to do, she does not reply. How would you assist Denise? Include at least four different strategies you might try. How would you have other children assist Denise?

b) From the moment he came through the door today, Timmy has been talking about the fish he and his dad caught yesterday. "I caught three fish, big ones. We dug worms. They eat 'em, and I felt tugs on my line. We couldn't stand because then the boat might tip. We skinned 'em and cut off the heads, and you could see inside what they ate. One just ate a crayfish. We opened his stomach and saw it . . ." How would you use Timmy's experience and enthusiasm to help him make a plan?

c) Suppose Timmy plans to play fisherman in the house area, but by the time he tells you his plan there are already five children in the house area playing doctor. What would you do? Include at least four different approaches you might try.

d) Raymond and Elise have planned to build a farm together in the block area. While you are still planning with other children, you are aware that, although Raymond and Elise have gone to the block area, they are not building a farm. Instead they are kneeling on the rubber animals to see how flat they can make them. Would you immediately leave the children you are still planning with and go to Elise and Raymond, or would you wait until everyone had made a plan and then go to the block area? Why?

e) Once you got to the block area, what might you say to Elise and Raymond? Think of at least four different strategies you might try.

7. Work time

You have just finished planning with the children in your planning group and are looking around the room to see what's going on. This is what you see:

Mike and Sam are going around the room noisily "chain sawing" blocks, chairs, table legs, the record player, the easel. Clarice and Michelle started out mixing the paints they needed for their pictures but are now pouring all the paint powder into one jar to see what color it will make. Raymond and Timmy are building a long road in the block area. Your co-teacher is doing puzzles with Elise, Sasha, and Corey. Denise is standing in the house area sucking her thumb, holding her dolly, and gazing around the room. Brenda and Jamison are dressing up as "the mom and the dad" and talking about going to work and cooking breakfast. Marketta is crying because Troy took two blocks she was starting to load into his dump truck. "Teacher, teacher," Lynnette is calling from the art area. "Look at my picture, look at my picture."

a) Where would you go first? Why? What would you do?

b) Where would you go next? Why? What would you do?

c) As you are going to your second situation, your co-teacher looks around. Where might your co-teacher go? Why? What might your co-teacher do?

d) Are there situations you did not get a chance to deal with? Which ones? What might you and your co-teacher discuss about these situations when planning tomorrow's work time?

8. Recall time

The work time described in exercise 7 has just ended. Clean-up time is over and you are recalling with Sasha, Denise, Timmy, Mike, Clarice, Raymond, Brenda, and Troy.

a) During clean-up time you made mental notes of each child's activity at work time (refer to exercise 7). List these activities.

Child	Activities
Sasha	
Denise	
Timmy	
Mike	
Clarice	
Raymond	
Brenda	
Troy	

b) Given the age, work-time activity, and brief description of each of these children, how would you conduct recall time? What questions would you ask? What objects would you have at the table? Would you ask children to go and get any objects?

9. Small-group time

You are planning a small-group time for Elise, Sam, Michelle, Corey, Jamison, Marketta, and Lynnette.

a) List everything you know about each of these children.

Child	Facts About Child
Elise	
Sam	
Michelle	
Corey	
Jamison	
Marketta	
Lynnette	

b) Choose a skill or key experience that will be the focus of your small-group time.

c) List the materials you will use and how many of each so that every child will have his or her own things to work with.

d) Where will this small-group activity take place so that everyone has enough work space?

e) What choices will children be able to make?

f) How will you begin this small-group activity? What will you say?

g) Describe what you might see each child doing during this activity and how you would support and encourage each child.

Child	Child's Actions with Materials	Strategies for Support and Encouragement
Elise		
Sam		
Michelle		
Corey		
Jamison		
Marketta		
Lynnette		

h) How would you draw this activity to a meaningful end?

10. Circle time

You are planning a circle time for the 15 children in your preschool.

a) List four activities (action games, songs, finger plays) you have done or would like to do with 15 preschoolers.

1.   3.

2.   4.

b) For each activity you listed, think about an active beginning, choices for children, and opportunities for children to lead. Record your plans in the chart below.

Activity	Active Beginning	Choices for Children	Opportunities for Children to Lead

11. Transition times

Review page 98 in **Young Children in Action** and then go back to exercise 3b. Read through the sequence you decided on for Elaine and Philip's day. Identify three transitions and describe strategies you would use to help children go smoothly from one time block to the next.

Transition	Strategies

12. Observing a daily routine

Visit a preschool classroom and spend a day observing the daily routine. Turn to the daily routine checklist on pages 298-303 of **Young Children in Action** and use it to evaluate the classroom.

a) List the components of the classroom's daily routine in the order in which they occur.

b) In the classroom you observed, how are the components and sequence of the daily routine similar to those described in **Young Children in Action** on pages 59-61? How are they different?

c) If you were a member of the teaching team in this classroom, what, if any, changes in the daily routine would you suggest? Why?

13. Daily routine issues to ponder

a) Should recalling occur only at recall time? Why or why not? When else during the daily routine could it occur?

b) Since children plan and carry out their own work-time activities, what is an adult's role during work time?

c) What is the effect of a consistent daily routine on a child from a chaotic household? From a rigid household? Would your expectations for two such children differ? How and why, or why not?

d) What impact does room arrangement have on daily routine?

e) Would it be easier to start the year with all new children who didn't know the daily routine, or with a mix of children—some who already knew the daily routine and some who didn't? Why?

f) How would you help a non-English-speaking child learn the daily routine?

g) What do you remember about the daily routine in the nursery school or kindergarten you attended as a child? What was your favorite time of the day? Your least favorite time? Why?

14. Daily routine projects

a) Try out some of the strategies to help children learn the daily routine you listed in exercise 4.

b) Make a daily routine book for a child. Take photographs of the child's day. Have the child dictate the text.

c) At least once a month, observe the same child going through the plan-do-review sequence. Make notes on each step and compare them from month to month.

d) Using the steps outlined in exercise 9, plan, do, and evaluate a small-group time with preschoolers.

e) Do and evaluate one of the circle-time activities you planned in exercise 10.

Films and Publications

Films

Guidelines for Evaluating Activities
[PS150] Set of three 16mm films; black & white, sound; 58 min total; discussion guides included
These programs demonstrate alternative ways teachers can plan and carry out activities with a group of preschool children. Each program shows two contrasting styles of structuring and leading a group activity using similar materials but different teaching methods and goals. Useful for stimulating discussion of teaching styles and educational philosophies. An accompanying observation guide offers criteria by which to evaluate and revise classroom activities. Also included is a trainer's supplement that discusses the films in terms of the criteria in the guide and offers suggestions for revising the activities.

Contrasting Teaching Styles: Small-Group Time
[PS151] (18 min)

Contrasting Teaching Styles: Work Time, the Art Area
[PS152] (22 min)

***Contrasting Teaching Styles: Circle Time** [PS153] (18 min)*

Helping Children Make Choices and Decisions
[PS100] Set of five 16mm films; color, sound; 33 min total

3. Exploring the Possibilities of the Room
[PS103] (7 min).
In order to make responsible and creative choices, children need to be aware of the alternatives available to them. Teachers demonstrate some ways to help young children explore the possibilities of the classroom—the many activities and materials to choose from and the many imaginative ways materials can be used.

Troubles and Triumphs at Home
[PS192] Set of four color filmstrips and cassettes; 70 min total
The materials are directed at parents of children with special needs, aged two to five, but they may be of interest to anyone who has child care responsibilities for young children. Many of the ideas and activities are appropriate for center-based as well as home settings. Instead of attempting to provide pat solutions, the materials present some general problem-solving approaches and show examples of how certain families have applied these approaches in their homes. The strategies shown are meant to be suggestions for parents—catalysts for helping them develop ideas and strategies of their own.

There are four sound filmstrips with both English and Spanish soundtracks; four booklets; and a guide for parent meetings. The print materials are designed to be photo-reproduced (xeroxed) so that copies can be distributed to viewers as handouts.

When "I've Told You A Thousand Times" Isn't Enough
[PS193] (16 min)
All parents of two- to five-year-olds have those difficult days when everything their child does seems designed to anger, frustrate, or embarrass them. But young children have a difficult time learning what is appropriate and what is not in various situations. They also have trouble predicting, planning for, and sequencing events. This filmstrip discusses three important strategies parents can use to minimize many child behavior problems: communicating adult expectations in concrete and understandable ways, enforcing limits consistently, and helping children predict and plan for what is coming next.

Observing in the Classroom
[PS184] (13 min)
Reassures parents that they have unique knowledge and resources to contribute in the classroom. Points out the materials and equipment in the classroom areas—block area, house area, art area, quiet area—and shows children as they are involved in the various parts of the daily routine: planning time, work time, clean-up time, recall time, outside time, small-group time, and circle time. Designed to help parents become comfortable with the classroom and routine as a first step toward volunteering in the classroom.

The Daily Routine
[EE201] 16mm film; color, sound; 30 min
A typical day in a cognitively oriented elementary classroom, with scenes from the High/Scope Elementary School. This film shows how a consistent routine can help children take a more self-directed, active approach to learning. The film documents the major components of the daily routine—planning and work time, clean-up, small-group and juice time, activity time and circle time—and discusses the purposes of each.

Your Baby's Day: A Time for Learning
[ID321] Color filmstrip/cassette; 12 min
Demonstrates appropriate activities for adults which will enhance babies' development through routine activities such as feeding, changing, and bathing. The program is designed to make parents aware of their vital role in a baby's development at three important stages: newborn, four to eight months, and eight months to a year. Useful for parents-to-be, for high school and community college courses in child development, for training adults in day care centers. Realistic, supportive suggestions for adult-infant interactions. Print guide included.

Publications

The Daily Routine
(#2, Elementary Series)
Author: S. Mainwaring; booklet (36 pages); 1975.
This guide is designed to help the teacher provide a consistent classroom routine which takes into account the child's need for active involvement and decision making and the teacher's need for an orderly setting. The important components of the daily routine are planning, working, representing, and evaluating. Strategies are provided for setting up the routine and helping children carry out this process. Some answers to common questions are included, as well as sample plans for children at different developmental levels and suggestions for teacher plans and evaluations.

The Daily Routine: Small-Group Times
(#9, Elementary Series)
Author: R. Lalli; booklet (80 pages); 1978.
This supplement to *The Daily Routine* contains guidelines for planning small-group instruction and gives suggestions for 100 sample group times. Topics covered are the relationship areas of space, classification, seriation, and time; language; mathematics; and the content areas of art, drama, construction, sewing, music, and movement. Descriptions include the key experiences and developmental level for which each activity is appropriate as well as suggested questions, materials, and extensions.

Write or call the High/Scope Foundation, 600 North River Street, Ypsilanti, MI 48197, (313) 485-2000 to obtain information on ordering these materials.

3/ Teaching in a team

In a classroom where children and adults work together as problem solvers, decision makers, planners, and doers, everyone depends on everyone else for support, encouragement, ideas, and assistance. In this environment, a cohesive teaching team is essential.

1. You as a team member

One way to assess how you might work as a member of a preschool teaching team is to assess your role in other working groups.

a) What group have you belonged to that has worked well together?

b) What was the major goal or purpose of this group?

c) How would you describe your role in this group?

d) When conflicts arose in this group, how were they resolved? What part did you play?

e) What was the most difficult thing you had to do as a member of this group?

f) What was most satisfying about being a member of this group?

g) What could have improved the way this group worked together?

2. An ideal teaching team

You are putting together a teaching team for your community-service preschool center. From among all your friends, relations, and acquaintances past and present, choose two people to teach with you. Consider your own strengths and limitations, the needs of three- and four-year-olds, and the need for a team that works well together.

a) Who would you choose and why?

b) Who might emerge as the leader of this team? Why?

c) How do you think this team would deal with disagreements among team members? For example, suppose that the three of you are discussing whether or not children should be allowed to go outside during work time. One person says yes; another says not unless an adult goes with them; and a third says, "No, they don't learn enough outside."

3. Setting up a real teaching team

Because this curriculum relies heavily on the collective energies, ideas, and support of a teaching team, teamwork becomes an important learning experience. With this in mind, find two people in your class who will work together with you as a teaching team as you do the exercises in this book.

a) Record the names of your team members and five biographical facts about each one.

Team Member	Biographical Facts
	1. 2. 3. 4. 5.
	1. 2. 3. 4. 5.

b) Review daily routine (Chapter 2, exercise 4). With your team members, agree on a daily routine for your team's preschool.

Time	Name of Time Block

c) Review room arrangement (Chapter 1, exercises 5 and 6). As a team, agree on a plan for a preschool classroom and an outdoor play space, incorporating suggestions from each team member. Draw your plan in the space below.

_____ Your Team's Classroom and Outdoor Play Space _____

d) Turn to **Young Children in Action,** page 102. Decide together on the common expectations for team members and record your decisions in the following chart:

Situation	Expectations
Leaving the room	
Talking across the room	
Maintaining contact	
Anger	
Talking about children	
Catastrophes	
Small-group time	
Staying or "floating"	
"Off" days	
Children's adult preferences	

4. Setting limits and expectations

You and your team members decided not to try to set limits and expectations for the children until you had a chance to see what they were like in the classroom. Well, today you saw!

Clarice came bursting in saying, "I don't wanna make a plan, I don't wanna make a plan." You were supposed to plan with her, but instead you let her go straight to the house area. Later when another adult asked her about her plan, she ran away into the block area.

Troy hauled out all the blocks, then left them in a pile and joined a fingerpainting group in the art area. At clean-up time, he helped with the fingerpaint clean up but wouldn't help with the blocks.

Brenda was playing house and needed some acorns for food, so she went outside to gather some from the tree in the yard. Lynnette left the art area when she saw Brenda outside and went outside with Brenda, taking a paint brush and a jar of paint with her to paint acorns. They didn't come in until after clean-up time.

During small-group time, Sam went to the bathroom and, on his way back, joined another small group. He wasn't disruptive but Jamison, when he saw Sam in another group, wanted to go too.

Since Raymond wasn't finished with his small-group time project, he didn't want to come to circle time. He stayed at the table working through circle time. Then Marketta joined him, followed by Clarice. Two adults left the circle to deal with these three children, leaving you with the rest of the children, who quickly got out of hand.

a) List the potential trouble spots that occurred throughout the day.

b) Considering these occurrences, together with your team members establish limits and expectations for the children in your classroom.

48

c) How would your teaching team communicate these new limits and expectations to the children?

5. Observing a teaching team at work

Go to a preschool classroom with your team members. Watch the teaching team in action and afterwards discuss the following questions together:

a) Do all team members arrive before the children? If not, what effect does the later arrival of some staff members seem to have?

b) What does each team member do before the children arrive?

c) What does each team member do throughout the daily routine?

d) What common expectations for themselves do team members seem to have?

e) What common limits and expectations does the team have for children?

6. Team issues to ponder

a) In a teaching team, is it necessary that one member function as a leader? Why or why not? Or should all team members function as peers? Why or why not? Should they designate a leader or let leaders evolve from time to time? Explain. Will different situations call for different leaders? Explain.

b) Under what kind of leadership style would you prefer to work—autocratic, laissez faire, democratic? Why? What kind of leader are you? How do you know?

c) Are there people in the world who cannot work as team members? Why or why not?

d) Think of a person you know who works well with one group but not with another. Why is this the case?

e) If you were an administrator in charge of a large new corporate day care center and you were faced with the task of dividing 12 adults into five teaching teams, how would you proceed? Would you involve the 12 people in the process? Why or why not, and if yes, how?

f) What would you do if one of your teaching-team members spoke very little English?

7. Team projects

a) As a team, select an upcoming topic from the class syllabus. Plan, carry out, and evaluate a presentation of the topic to the rest of the class. Make sure your presentation involves the class members in active-learning experiences.

b) As a team, observe a preschool classroom. Select four children to observe. After observing, pool your information, listing everything you observed about the four children—their strengths, developmental levels, interests—and tell each other what you might do with each child if you had the opportunity.

c) As a team, buy a model airplane and assemble it together. Afterwards, talk about how you worked together as a team.

Films and Publications

Films

Team Planning in the Cognitively Oriented Curriculum

[PS160] 16mm film; black & white; 18 min
This film documents the activities of two preschool teachers at various times of the school day. It shows them planning, considering ways to support both the children and each other, sharing observations of the children, and evaluating the effectiveness of the activities they had planned for the day.

Publications

Planning by Teachers *(#4)*
Author: L. Ransom: booklet (44 pages); 1978
This practical handbook sets forth guidelines for a teaching team's organization and implementation of a unified classroom program. Included in the book are suggested techniques and sample forms for child observation and record keeping, strategies for planning daily and long-term classroom activities, and a list of curriculum resources available from High/Scope Foundation. Appendices show sample forms for teacher self-evaluation and reports to parents, as well as the "Key Experiences K-6" for children and the High/Scope "Child Observation Record K-6."

Write or call the High/Scope Foundation, 600 North River Street, Ypsilanti, MI 48197, (313) 485-2000 to obtain information on ordering these materials.

4/Planning in a team

Daily team planning focuses on specific elements of the curriculum framework. The curriculum framework gives adults both a way to observe children's actions in relation to their intellectual development and a range of possible ways to support and extend their interests and actions. Team planning at the end of each day gives teaching-team members the opportunity to report and assess their classroom observations and to plan what they are going to do about them.

The exercises in this chapter are designed to be done with your team members. The teaching team referred to in this chapter and throughout the rest of this book is the team composed of you and two people in your class (the team formed in Chapter 3). Before proceeding with the exercises, find all the blanks in this and the next chapter and together decide whose name to write in.

Figure 1 on pages 54-59 contains observations you and your teaching team made of one day in your community-service preschool classroom. The exercises ask you to make plans based on the information in these observations.

On the day these observations were made, you each planned a different activity for small-group time:

_____'s group   Using playdough, toothpicks, and pipe cleaners

_____'s group   Finding and stringing things with holes

_____'s group   Building with small colored blocks

The circle-time activity was singing "Everybody Do This Just Like Me" and having each child, in turn, say or show an action for everyone to do.

Figure 1

Planning Time	Work Time	Clean-up Time
BRENDA (4½) Dictated plan to play in house area, dress up, cook, go to store with Jamison.	Followed plan. Helped Jamison with buttons and tie. Used acorns, styrofoam, buttons, for food. Sorted them into muffin tins. Went to store in block area. Directed Denise and Jamison in building of a store. Had _____ take a Polaroid picture of store. Did some counting using blocks for money.	Enjoyed sorting acorns, styrofoam, buttons, into cannisters. Helped with block area.
CLARICE (3) Just said, "Art Area—paint" and went right over to get started.	Spent a lot of time mixing and stirring paints. (She would probably like a water table.) Finally got to painting on easel. Made drip design, then covered whole paper solidly with paint. When asked to tell about her picture, she said, "Storm, nighttime, big rain."	Spent whole time washing brushes.
COREY (3½) "Finish my plane at the workbench."	Added lots of nails and bottle caps to plane. "These are wheels. These are where the men sit. These are smoke coming out. These are for blast off." When he started flying plane around workbench, _____ asked him what he would like to do next with his plane. "Show my dad." _____ suggested painting it or building an airport for it. He decided to paint it which took the rest of work time.	Washed brushes with Clarice. Got silly but was able to redirect energies to sponging off tables.
DENISE (3) No response at all to "What would you like to do today?" So _____ asked if Denise would like to go with _____ to an area to see what was there. Denise nodded yes. When asked which area, she pointed to the quiet area. So they went there together.	They looked at shelf together. In response to "Is there anything on this shelf you'd like to play with?" she pointed to the inch cubes. She piled and filled and emptied with these as long as _____ was with her. When _____ started to leave she wanted to come too. _____ pulled out the beads and the cuisinaire rods and these held her attention long enough for _____ to leave. Later she joined _____ in the block area where she stacked, piled, filled, emptied with small, colored blocks. Brought blocks to Jamison for store.	Did not really do much cleaning up. Picked up a few blocks, then stopped.
ELISE (4½) Drew picture of blocks, farm animals, and traced over the words " block area" that _____ wrote.	Built an elaborate farm with Raymond, including house, two barns, fences, pastures, and roads. Some dispute when Brenda and Jamison came to build store because farm took up so much room. _____ sat them all down together, and they decided that store could be along the farm road. Farmers bought things from store.	Used some of clean-up time to draw a picture of farm "to share."

Figure 1 (continued)

Recall Time	Small-Group Time	Circle Time	Outside Time
Talked about Polaroid picture of store. Other kids wanted to see if they were in the picture.	Built store shelves with playdough and toothpicks. Used pipe cleaners for "moms" and "store people."	Late to circle because she wanted to finish her store for her mom when she came to pick her up. Had idea of pretending to skate.	Gathered acorns and stones and sorted them into two different bags. Again, involved Denise in this activity.
"I painted." Enjoyed showing her picture and having "story" read.	Did not find things with holes. Worked just with wooden beads, rolling and piling them. Did some sorting by color.	When it was her turn to suggest a way to move, repeated clapping we had just done.	Played in sandbox, filling and emptying. Ran out of containers.
Showed his plane. Repeated explanation for each part.	Added playdough to his plane. Toothpicks were "driving sticks." Didn't want to take things off his plane at end but if he took his playdough home, everyone else would want to. Finally took it off.	Had everyone move like a plane.	Flew his plane off the climber. _____ worked with him to find a place where it wouldn't fly into people. Also flew other things off climber: paper, sticks, cardboard box, grass. Talked about which things were heavier and how they flew.
Said nothing but did go to get inch cubes and nodded in agreement when _____ talked about what she had done.	Sat next to Clarice, rolling and piling beads. Did not talk to Clarice even though they were engaged in same activity with same materials.	Wouldn't suggest a movement, just covered her face with her hands, so others covered their faces with their hands. She seemed to like this.	Stayed by _____, then joined Clarice filling a bag with acorns. Took hers home.
Used picture to tell others about her farm. _____ helped use location words like "next to," "inside of," "behind," rather than just "here."	Used blocks to build a symmetrical building with fence around it. Worked a long time to make the fence square. Wanted each side to be the same.	Had so many ideas she had a hard time waiting for her turn.	Made a house in the bushes with Lynnette and Raymond. Used leaves for food, stones for money. Bought acorns from Brenda.

55

Figure 1 (continued)

Planning Time	Work Time	Clean-up Time
JAMISON (4) Planned to "play with Brenda in the house area. I'm gonna be the dad."	Spent a long time lining up ties next to each other to find the longest because, as dad, he needed "the biggest one." Then worked on knot in front of mirror. Finally called Brenda: "Honey, you gotta tie this pesky knot." Got angry at Elise and Raymond for taking up so much room in the block area. Threatened to knock down farm so he could build store. _____ stepped in before they came to blows. Jamison actually came up with the solution: build store next to the road so farmers could come to store too. Didn't really want Denise to help until he realized that he needed her blocks.	Disappeared into the bathroom at clean-up time, so others left the ties for him to put away.
LYNNETTE (4½) "Paint, paint, paint. I wanna paint a big picture for my dad."	Tore off big piece of butcher paper; tried to put it on the easel but it was too big. Put it on the floor but Clarice kept walking on it to get to sink. Finally put it on table. Clarice was using all the containers to mix paint in and Lynnette was getting frustrated so _____ stepped in and asked if there were other containers she could think of. She got a muffin tin from the house area that no one was using. Asked Clarice to pour some paint into her muffin tin. Painted elaborate mural with house, family members, barbecue, bikes. Dictated story.	Had to find space where her big picture could dry undisturbed—outside in sun. Used rocks for weights. When her brushes were cleaned, helped in block area.
MARKETTA (3) Pointed to quiet area and said, "Puzzles."	Went right to rabbit puzzle and did it two or three times. Then tried farm puzzle which she had never done before. Worked alone for a long time until she got it, then called _____ over to see it. Didn't say much, but very pleased. At _____'s suggestion, traced around each puzzle piece and labeled it so she could show her mom. Afterwards on her own she traced rabbit puzzle pieces.	Put away puzzles. Helped with blocks.
MICHELLE (4½) Drew plans for birdhouse she wanted to make at workbench. Labeled "Top, sides, bottom."	Took plan with her. Found wood that was near length of lines on her plan. Pounded, glued, sawed, drilled, added bottle caps "for places to hold the food in." Talked with Corey a lot.	Cleaned up, straightened workbench.
MIKE (3) Wanted to "Saw, brrum, cut down trees." He meant he wanted to pretend to chain saw. _____ talked about how that disturbed other children and suggested sawing with hand saw at workbench. Mike agreed, but planned to chain saw outside at outside time.	Spent quite a lot of time choosing a "big, big piece of wood" and then fitting it into the vice. Needed help getting his cut started but kept going to the end, once started. Sawed two-by-four into five "woods" or blocks. Intrigued by sawdust.	Carefully swept sawdust into box so he could save it.

Figure 1 (continued)

Recall Time	Small-Group Time	Circle Time	Outside Time
Missed because putting away ties.	Found all kinds of things with holes to string. Made pattern: red bead, spool, button, Tinkertoy.	Had everyone move like a dinosaur and then like a bulldozer.	Played football with _____ and Timmy. Accurate thrower and catcher.
Had her group go outside to see picture and read story. Elise indicated that she wanted to make a big picture tomorrow.	Used blocks to make a family on a picnic.	Had everyone pretend they were painting.	House in bushes with Elise and Raymond.
Showed puzzle tracings. Named each part.	Lined her blocks up, some according to shape, some according to color. "Long lines" was her explanation.	Touched her head, touched her knees.	Wanted pushing on the swing. Cried when _____ had her work on pumping.
Showed birdhouse. Said she wanted to make birds for her house in art area "so real birds know where to come."	Used playdough and pipe cleaners to make birds. Got involved in seeing how small a bird she could make.	Had everyone jump up and down; jump and turn; go into the circle and back out again.	Used swings, climbed swing-set pole, and slid down. Surprised herself that she could climb so high. Troy saw her and together they were firemen.
Brought wood pieces over and showed how he sawed them. Also showed sawdust.	Used blocks to build towers and knock them down. Said his hand was a "chain saw cutting the blocks down."	Had everyone jump up and down every time it was his turn to suggest a motion.	Played chain saw with Sam. Found some tall weeds they could easily knock down. Got involved in seeing how big a pile of weeds they could make. Then piled them into a wagon.

Figure 1 (continued)

Planning Time	Work Time	Clean-up Time
RAYMOND (4) Dictated plan to work in block area building a farm with Elise.	(See work time notes on Elise) In addition, Raymond loaded all the farm animals into the truck to take to "the place where they get made into meat." Tried various-sized trucks until he found one where they'd all fit.	Used truck to drive blocks back to shelves. Spent a lot of time fitting blocks into truck.
SAM (3) As usual, wanted to "work with Mike." _____ suggested that he make two plans: first, something *he'd* like to do and second, working with Mike. Looked around, saw Clarice in art area and said, "Work with Clarice."	Mixed, stirred, and poured paint with Clarice, then spent rest of work time painting at easel. Never did go to work with Mike although he periodically went to look at Mike's sawing.	Hung his picture, helped with brushes, then helped Mike sweep sawdust.
SASHA (3½) During planning time, left his group, went to quiet area, and dumped all the puzzles upside down. _____ joined him, said, "Looks like you planned to work with puzzles today." Sasha nodded enthusiastically.	Couldn't begin to put puzzles together, too many pieces all jumbled together. So first they turned all pieces right-side-up. _____ gave him the animal puzzle board and played "Can you find the . . . ?" _____ named the animal; Sasha found the puzzle piece and worked to get it into the board. After he finished the animal puzzle, he wanted to do it again, so he did. Third time, he did it without help. _____ started to put the rest of the puzzle pieces back but Sasha said no and proceeded to stack and pile them like blocks.	Could not put puzzles back together, but did help put finished puzzles back in rack.
TIMMY (4½) Planned to make "fish I can really catch" in the art area. Talked about different materials he could use so they would actually hook on his pole. Decided on paper clips on pole and hole in fish.	Found stick outside. Tied string to stick and paper clip onto string for pole. Used construction paper for fish. Punched hole near mouth but when he put fish on floor and tried to catch it, couldn't get paper clip "hook" into mouth. "Hey, teacher, this don't work." In response to "What else could you try?" he thought of using tape loops or "bending paper clips up on the fish's mouth." Tried both. Paper clip idea worked best. Made "pond" out of blue paper. Used Tinkertoys for sticks to build a fire to cook fish. Gave fish to farmers in block area for supper.	No trouble putting his things away, then helping in block area.
TROY (3) Planned to "cook over there" pointing to the house area. Would not elaborate so _____ said she'd be over later to try some of his cooking.	Played next to Brenda, but not with her and Jamison. Mostly filled, emptied coffee pot which he worked on awhile, getting all the parts together properly. Used buttons, acorns, poker chips. Stirred, poured from pan to pan. When _____ saw that he really wasn't pretending to cook but was manipulating the materials, _____ asked him to pour some buttons, which he did. Poured till all the cups were full. "Lots and lots." Together they counted 10.	Very intrigued sorting buttons and poker chips back into their containers.

Figure 1 (continued)

Recall Time	Small-Group Time	Circle Time	Outside Time
Brought truck and animals to show how they all fit into truck.	Used different-sized washers to string "from the tiniest to the biggest." Was able to maintain pattern by himself.	Missed most of circle because he was tracing around his washer necklace so he could show his mom and dad.	Made a house with Elise and Lynnette. "I'll do the heavy things cause I'm the dad." Pushed logs over to make the sides. Wanted to pile to make "log cabin," but logs kept rolling off.
Showed his picture. "It's a big thing. It's scary."	Rolled snakes. The big snakes ate the little snakes.	Had everyone clap hands, clap knees.	(See Mike at outside time.)
Wouldn't say or show what he did, so _____ told group how he did the animal puzzle.	Worked with playdough whole time. Patted, pounded, rolled, licked, smelled, stuck toothpicks in, squished.	Kept leaving circle to go back to playdough. Finally sat on _____'s lap.	Played in sandbox, pouring water into sand.
Demonstrated his fishing pole. Other children intrigued.	Put all the same things together on his string—red beads, then big washers, then blue buttons, then yellow beads, finally small washers.	Suggested pretending to cast a fishing pole, swimming, kicking feet.	Football with _____ and Jamison. Learning to catch. Good thrower and runner.
"I made 10 cups to the top." Proud of knowing number.	Made piles and stacks of blocks, sometimes all of same color or shape. Did some fitting of square blocks into a shoe box to cover up the bottom. "See my floor."	Had others shake their hands then their feet.	Played in sandbox near Sasha. Not much interaction, however.

1. Organizing planning sessions around key experiences

One way a teaching team can approach the planning process is by looking at what children are doing with regard to the key experiences. Turn to pages 3-6 in **Young Children in Action** for a complete list of the key experiences.

a) As you read through Figure 1, list the key experiences that children were experiencing on the day the observations were made. An example is given.

Time of Day	Key Experiences
Planning Time	*choosing materials, activities, purposes*
Work Time	
Clean-up Time	
Recall Time	
Small-Group Time	
Circle Time	
Outside Time	

60

b) Using the format outlined on pages 106-11 in **Young Children in Action,** make a plan for the day after the observations in Figure 1 were made. Choose the key experiences you want to work on and think of strategies and activities that would support and extend the activities noted in the observations.

Time of Day	Key Experiences	Strategies and Activities
Planning Time		
Work Time		
Clean-up Time		
Recall Time		
_____'s Small-Group Time		
_____'s Small-Group Time		
_____'s Small-Group Time		
Circle Time		
Outside Time		

2. Organizing planning sessions around the daily routine

Another way to use your day's observations to plan for the next day is to look carefully at each segment of the daily routine to determine the issues you want to work on and the strengths you want to support. Refer to the observations in Figure 1 to answer the following questions:

a) How did the children indicate their plans? List the different ways.

b) How would you plan to support or extend, tomorrow or some time in the near future, each way of planning?

c) Which three children would you pick to be particularly aware of during work time tomorrow? Why? How would you support or extend their activities?

d) Which two children seem to need help at clean-up time? How would you work with them at clean-up time tomorrow?

e) List the children in your small group and describe what each one did with the materials.

Child	Use of Materials

f) Considering the information just listed, what small-group time activity would you plan for your group of children tomorrow to support and extend each child's interests and abilities? Briefly describe the activity, the materials available to each child, and how you predict each child would use them.

Activity

Materials

Child	Possible Responses

g) Brenda, Denise, Elise, Raymond, and Sasha each experienced particular difficulties at circle time. What were they? How would you plan to deal with these issues tomorrow at circle time?

Child	Circle-Time Problem	Strategies for Tomorrow
Brenda		
Denise		
Elise		
Raymond		
Sasha		

h) How would you deploy yourselves at outside time tomorrow, assuming that it was very similar to the outside time recorded in the observations in Figure 1. Which children would you work with? How? (For a diagram of your outdoor area, refer to page 13.)

3. Organizing planning sessions around individual children

As part of their daily planning sessions, some teaching teams talk about five or six children and record specific observations and strategies to try the next day.

a) Review pages 113-20 in **Young Children in Action.** Then fill out the following chart, using the information in the observations in Figure 1. You may not be able to fill in every box for every child. You may also want to refer to the list of key experiences on pages 3-6 in **Young Children in Action.**

Assessment of Children's Actions and Language

	Representation	Classification	Seriation or Number Concepts	Spatial or Temporal Relations
Clarice				
Corey				
Jamison				
Lynnette				
Marketta				
Timmy				
Troy				

b) Pick one of the seven children and plan how you would support and extend his or her actions and language in each area.

Child: _____

Area	Support Strategies
Representation	
Classification	
Seriation or Number Concepts	
Spatial or Temporal Relations	

4. Planning for special events

Periodically, team planning for the next day is influenced by an upcoming event or holiday. At such times it is important to make plans that strike a balance between children's current activities and interests and new activities that relate to the special event. Some ways to strike this balance are to think of event-related materials to make available for children to choose to use at work time; to plan event-related, small-group activities that will allow each child to work at his or her own level; and to modify favorite circle-time activities to relate in some way to the event (singing "Old MacDonald Had a Halloween Party," for example, and naming all the kinds of people who came to it).

The day after the observations in Figure 1 were made is the day before Thanksgiving. You and your team members are planning with this special event in mind.

a) What Thanksgiving-related materials would you add to the work areas for children to use at work time tomorrow?

Area	Materials
House	
Block	
Art	
Quiet	

b) What Thanksgiving-related, small-group activity would you plan so that each child had materials to work with at his or her own level? Describe the activity, the materials, and how each child might respond.

Activity   **Materials for Each Child**

Child	Possible Responses

5. Planning for field trips and follow-up activities

Ideas for field trips often emerge from children's interests and activities. In the example given in **Young Children in Action,** pages 122-23, the teaching team plans a field trip to a gas station because they have observed children playing gas station quite a bit during work time. In this exercise you will be examining your children's interests and planning a field trip around them.

a) Read through the observations in Figure 1 and pick out an interest and a corresponding place to visit.

Interest   **Place to Visit**

b) When during the day will you make this visit?

c) What active things would you like children to be able to do on this visit?

d) Upon returning to the classroom on the day of the visit, how would you help the children recall the visit?

e) What new, visit-related materials would you add to the classroom the next day?

Area   **Materials**

f) How else would you follow up the visit?

6. Observing team planning

Observe a teaching team as they plan, using the checklist on pages 303-4 in **Young Children in Action** as you observe.

a) If you were in a position to give this teaching team feedback on their planning process, what strengths would you identify?

b) What problem areas in their planning process might you identify? Give possible solutions.

7. Team planning issues to ponder

a) Some people think it is easier to plan alone and that team planning is a waste of time and energy. What do you think and why?

b) Some people think that daily team planning is unnecessary and that weekly planning is sufficient. What do you think and why?

c) Since children make their own plans in this curriculum, why is team planning necessary at all?

d) Where do you think the major planning emphasis lies in this curriculum—in team planning for activities or in team planning for children? Why?

e) Some people enjoy the give and take of teamwork and some people find it tedious. How do you feel about teamwork?

f) Once a team makes plans, to what extent should it stick to them? Under what circumstances might a team change its daily plan in midstream?

g) What are the major strengths of your teaching team?

8. Team planning projects

a) Join an actual teaching team for daily planning. Note the planning approach and how plans are made for individual children.

b) Observe or participate in the planning, carrying out, and evaluation of a special preschool event—a holiday, birthday, or other celebration.

c) Observe or participate in the planning, carrying out, and evaluation of a preschool field trip.

Films and Publications

Films

Team Planning in the Cognitively Oriented Curriculum
[PS160] 16mm film; black & white; 18 min
This film documents the activities of two preschool teachers at various times of the school day. It shows them planning, considering ways to support both the children and each other, sharing observations of the children, and evaluating the effectiveness of the activities they had planned for the day.

Guidelines for Evaluating Activities
[PS150] Set of three 16mm films; black & white, sound; 58 min total; discussion guides included
These programs demonstrate alternative ways teachers can plan and carry out activities with a group of preschool children. Each program shows two contrasting styles of structuring and leading a group activity, using similar materials but different teaching methods and goals. Useful for stimulating discussion of teaching styles and educational philosophies. An accompanying observation guide offers criteria by which to evaluate and revise classroom activities. Also included is a trainer's supplement that discusses the films in terms of the criteria in the guide and offers suggestions for revising the activities.

Contrasting Teaching Styles: Small-Group Time
[PS151] (18 min)

Contrasting Teaching Styles: Work Time, the Art Area
[PS152] (22 min)

Contrasting Teaching Styles: Circle Time
[PS153] (18 min)

The Block Area
[PS191] Set of five color filmstrips and cassette tapes; 38.7 min total

5. Observing a Child in the Block Area *(7 min)*
Lynnette builds a large structure in the block area and a teacher observes and works with her. The narrator discusses the kinds of questions a teacher might ask in this situation and the strategies she could use to help Lynnette extend and represent her structure.

Experiencing and Representing
[PS110] Set of four 16mm films; color, sound; 48 min total
These programs demonstrate the importance of direct experience and representational play and show how the preschool environment can promote both experience and representation. In each section two teachers discuss specific activities from their classroom and demonstrate a variety of teaching strategies.

Thinking and Reasoning in Preschool Children
[PS138] 16mm film; black & white, sound; 23 min
An overview of the characteristics of children's thinking in the "preoperational" stage of development. The film illustrates some of the important concepts and reasoning abilities that children develop during the preschool years. It shows how the child's understanding of the world affects his behavior and problem-solving methods. A concise introduction to a complex subject.

Key Experiences for Intellectual Development During the Preschool Years
[PS137] 16mm film; color, sound; 19 min
Scenes from the High/Scope Preschool illustrate some of the major "key experiences" for the cognitive development of the preschool-age child—in active learning, language, representation, classification, seriation, number concepts, temporal relations, and spatial relations.

Publications

Planning by Teachers *(#4)*
Author: L. Ransom; booklet (44 pages), 1978
This practical handbook sets forth guidelines for a teaching team's organization and implementation of a unified classroom program. Included in the book are suggested techniques and sample forms for child observation and record keeping, strategies for planning daily and long-term classroom activities, and a list of curriculum resources available from High/Scope Foundation. Appendices show sample forms for teacher self-evaluation, reports to parents, as well as the "Key Experiences K-6" for children and the High/Scope "Child Observation Record K-6."

Write or call the High/Scope Foundation, 600 North River Street, Ypsilanti, MI 48197, (313) 485-2000 to obtain information on ordering these materials.

5/Active learning

Action is doing—children doing. Action is handling, changing, moving, making things—not just watching. Action is sawing, sanding, hammering. Action is painting, making models of real things, mixing paints, learning to use the brush, covering the table with newspaper, discovering that bottle caps can be wheels. Action is squishing, pressing, rubbing, getting down on the floor, racing, pushing, comparing. Action is climbing up, spinning around, holding on, yelling with all your might. Action is shaking, making different sounds. It's filling, emptying, pouring, spilling, choosing, putting things together, balancing, making something as long as you can make it. Action is pretending to fly like a bird, be an elephant, drive a car. Action is pouring your own juice, tasting, feeling, touching, exploring all by yourself. Action is using your entire body to learn.

1. Active learning: For everyone

Things that people of all ages really know about are things they have actually done or experienced.

a) After reading the following paragraph about paper bags, list all the "academic" facts about paper bags imparted to you by this description.

Paper bags were invented in France just before the turn of the century by Petrus de la Papier. Using a coarse white paper made from discarded envelopes and scraps of linen from his wife Celeste's sewing basket, de la Papier folded the first paper bags in the shape of a rectangle and held them together with a strong, resinous glue. These first paper bags caught on like wild fire, and soon de la Papier expanded his line to include bags of various sizes and shapes, as well as bags with bottoms and handles. Today paper bags are made and used throughout the world to carry almost anything under the sun from socks to cylinders, from gadgets to groceries. In some countries they are also used to make Halloween masks and as food for commercially grown night crawlers.

b) Find a real paper bag and explore it for at least five minutes. Find out what it looks like, feels like, smells like, sounds like; find out how many things you can do with it. Then make a list of "experiential" facts about paper bags.

c) If you wanted preschoolers to learn as much as possible about paper bags, how would you help them do it?

d) Briefly decribe active-learning experiences you recall from your own childhood.

2. Recognizing the key experiences in active learning

Preschoolers are involved in active learning much of the time, but not all adults recognize active learning when they see it. In this exercise you will read descriptions of everyday situations and identify them with one or more of the following key experiences for active learning:

Key Experiences: Active Learning

- Exploring actively with all the senses

- Discovering relations through direct experience

- Manipulating, transforming, and combining materials

- Choosing materials, activities, purposes

- Acquiring skills with tools and equipment

- Using the large muscles

- Taking care of one's own needs

---

a) Mike had been cutting long strips of construction paper and decided he wanted to hold them together to make a book. He tried tape but the middle strips kept falling out, so he decided to use the stapler, pushed down on the top, then pulled the papers out to see the staple. He couldn't see the staple so he repeated the process, this time hitting the stapler harder. Again, no staple. This time he bent down so he could see if the staple was coming out. He pushed down slowly, saw the staple coming out, and finally realized that it didn't go into the paper because the paper was *under* the stapler rather than "between the jaws." Finally, he moved the papers between the jaws, pushed, and was delighted to see that the staple had gone through all the papers. Fifteen staples later he was satisfied that his book would stay together.
Identify the key experience(s).

b) At outside time, Michelle, Corey, and Raymond decided to build a "big house." They spent most of the time hauling logs and boards, rolling and pushing tree stumps and rocks together. Sometimes it took all of them together to push or carry or lift one stump. "You have to be strong to build a strong house," Raymond announced.
Identify the key experience(s).

c) When _____'s group arrived at the table for small-group time, they found an exciting selection of materials: bowl-shaped grapefruit rinds, straws, toothpicks, yarn, construction paper, pipe cleaners.

"I'm gonna make a nest," announced Elise, getting a rind and some straw.

"Mine's gonna be an Easter basket with this for a handle," said Lynnette, twisting together some pipe cleaners.

Marketta selected a rind, turned it rind-side-up, and began to poke toothpicks into it. Mike liked Marketta's idea and added yarn around his toothpicks to make "flags." Troy took some of everything to see how much would fit into his "bowl."

Identify the key experience(s).

d) "Look at my new mittens. My grandma made them. See, they have a *J* on them. That's for me, Jamison." After showing his new mittens to all his teachers, Jamison returned to the coat rack, took off his mittens (carefully tucking them into his pocket), removed and hung up his jacket, and sat down to work on his boots. After struggling, he called, "Hey teacher, these is stuck." _____ showed him how to grab the back of his shoe with one hand and the heel of his boot with the other and then asked Jamison to do the other boot the same way. "Look, I did it and my shoe stayed on!" exclaimed Jamison, and he put his boots under his jacket and headed off to make his plan.

Identify the key experience(s).

e) Denise had filled and emptied every container in the block area, so you brought in a large basket which Denise filled, carried, emptied, beat on the bottom, and rolled.

Identify the key experience(s).

f) Lynnette was building an "up and down" race track for the wind-up race car she got for her birthday. The flat part of the track was fine but the car kept jumping off the track because the hill she built was too steep. In her frustration, she knocked the hill down, turning it into a gradual rise. When her car made it all the way up to the top, she called you over and said, "Look, watch! My car goes up."

"So it does," you responded, "because you made your hill a little lower. Your first hill was too high. Can you make another hill?" Lynnette built two more hills into her track, testing and adjusting them until the car could traverse each one without falling off.

Identify the key experience(s).

g) A group of children were making playdough with you. "Ooo, look at all this sugar. We gonna use this, teacher?" asked Brenda. "I'm gonna taste it. . . yuck that ain't no sugar, that's salt. Yuck!"

"My salt feels like sand but my flour is very, very soft," announced Michelle.

"Sticky, sticks to my fingers like glue," commented Corey as he stirred the ingredients together in his bowl.

Sasha was smelling his playdough—"Ummmm." Then he tasted a bit. "No," he said, and spit it out.

"It smelled good but it didn't taste good. Is that it, Sasha?" you asked. He nodded his head enthusiastically.

Identify the key experience(s).

3. Child study: Observing an active learner

For this exercise and the subsequent child-study exercises in this book, you will need a three- or four-year-old child whom you can observe and work with periodically for about 30 minutes each time.

Child's Name: _____   Date: _____

Child's Age: _____   Location: _____

a) Watch the child for the first five or ten minutes, noting the following:

1. What is the child doing?

2. What key experience(s) of active learning is/are involved?

3. What choices is the child making?

4. What, if any, words is the child using to describe his or her actions?

5. How can you support this child's play?

b) Try out your ideas for supporting the child's play and describe the results.

4. Ingredients for active learning

Many teachers believe that as long as children are handling material, they are engaged in active learning. Manipulation of materials is essential, of course, but by itself it does not constitute active learning. Active learning occurs when all the following ingredients are present:

- *Materials* for each child
- *Manipulation* of those materials
- *Choice* by the child of what to try with which materials
- *Words* chosen and used by the child to describe what he or she is doing
- *Support* by adults or peers in the form of recognition or questions that help the child think about his or her actions

a) Read the following descriptions of situations that occur in your preschool classroom.

Situation A

Clarice is painting at the easel. She has chosen five colors and selected a brush for each color. She starts with red and very carefully paints a line from top to bottom on the left-hand side of the paper. Next to it she very carefully paints a blue line, and so on, until she has five colored lines next to each other. She starts over again with the blue brush and continues till the whole paper is filled with colored lines.

Situation B

_____'s small group is making Halloween masks. _____ gives each child a shoebox containing scissors, string, a piece of black construction paper, a piece of aluminum foil, paste, and some elbow macaroni. "Now," _____ begins, "I want each of you to choose something from your box that's black. Good, Clarice, you got the black paper. Good, Timmy. No, Denise, the scissors are not black, they're silver. Put them back and find something black." After each child has removed the black paper, _____ has them "choose something long and pointy." Once each child has found scissors, _____ shows everyone how to cut out eyes, nose, and mouth; glue macaroni for eyebrows; make an aluminum foil mustache; and attach a string to hold the mask on. "Good," _____ praises the children. "Let's wear our masks to circle time to show the other children."

Situation C

At circle time, you are reading a book about zoo animals. You hold up the first picture showing some children leaning over the fence watching a mother camel wash her baby. "Who can tell me about this picture?" you ask.
"That little girl shouldn't be standing at the fence. She might get bit," says Brenda.
"Her mamma's gonna give her a spanking when she gets home." Michelle adds.
"You're right. You shouldn't stand on the fence at the zoo," you say.
"My dad won't let us stand on our fence 'cause then the cows might get out and my mom has to chase 'em," Timmy says.
"You have cows at your house?" Michelle asks Timmy incredulously. "In the backyard?"
"Yep," Timmy replies. "Big ones and little ones."
"Does he, Teacher?" Brenda asks.
"Yes, Timmy lives in the country," you assure her.
"Coo, coo, coo," shouts Sasha, walking over to you and banging at the camel in the picture.

"I can't see, I can't see" call the other children as you help Sasha find his seat again.

"That ain't no cuckoo," Elise replies in disgust to Sasha. "That ain't no bird, that's a real big dog with a baby."

"Well, it does look like a dog," you say, picking up on Elise's comment. . .

Situation D

Corey and Sam are busy making roads and driving cars and trucks around in the sand table. They decide they need a tunnel for their cars to drive through, so they scrape together a big pile of sand and begin digging through it with spoons. "Hey, the sand keeps falling down," Sam tells Corey.

"They pile the sand back up, try again, and when the sand "falls down" again, they begin hitting it as hard as they can. Pretty soon they've forgotten about the tunnel and sand is flying in all directions as they chant, "The sand is falling down. The sand is falling down."

_____ comes over. "Hey, what are you guys doing? What's happening to your roads?" _____ asks.

"The sand is falling down," giggle the two boys. "Yes, I can see that. It's getting all over the floor," _____ responds. "What were you doing before the sand got all over the floor?"

"The sand fell down on the tunnel," Sam reports.

"Show me," _____ replies, and the two boys show _____ their problem. "What could you add to the sand to help keep it together, to help keep it from falling?" _____ asks, fully expecting "water" for an answer.

"Blocks?" Sam suggests.

"Well, get some and see."

Sam and Corey build a small tunnel with blocks and cover it with sand. "Look, teacher, the blocks are holding up the sand."

"They sure are. What a good idea," says _____ admiringly.

By the end of work time, Corey and Sam have built a number of tunnels using blocks, boxes, and paper towel tubes. _____ asks them to show and tell about their tunnels at recall time.

On the chart below, check the ingredients for active learning that are present in each situation.

Situation	Materials	Manipulation	Choice	Words	Support
A: Lines					
B: Masks					
C: Zoo book					
D: Tunnels					

b) Pick out the three situations from which the most ingredients for active learning are missing, and briefly describe how you would add these ingredients to each situation.

Situation	Missing Ingredients	Ways to Add Each Ingredient

c) How does a well-organized classroom arrangement contribute to active learning?

5. Active learning: Solving problems

Elise is washing her hands at clean-up time, and after making the sink stopper go up and down several times, she asks you, "Teacher, why does this thing keep the water in?"

You tell her, "Because when you pull up on the lever, the stopper covers the hole."

The next day at the sink she asks you, "Teacher, tell me again about the stopper." You repeat your explanation with a little bit of the I-already-told-you-once tone creeping into your voice.

When she repeats her question on the third day you reply in exasperation, "How do *you* think it works, Elise?" Falteringly she begins to put the process into her own words, and together you examine the rods and levers under the sink that activate the stopper. Elise is so excited about what she has learned that soon she has four or five other children looking under the sink and realizing what happens when they push the lever on top of the sink to close the drain.

To learn, the learner must often answer his or her own questions. Adults help children learn by helping them work through a problem rather than supplying them with the answers.

Following are brief descriptions of potential active-learning situations that adults have missed. In each situation, you could do something differently to turn the situation into a problem-solving experience, and thus a real learning experience, for the child.

a) Denise is trying to hang up her raincoat, but the coat hook is too high. After a while she gives up and just stands near the coat rack holding her raincoat and sucking her thumb. When _____ asks, "Do you need some help, Denise?" she nods yes, and _____ hangs her raincoat up for her.

What is your active-learning approach to the "Hook-Is-Too-High" problem?

b) Sasha is sitting in the middle of the block area grunting and waving his arms toward the block shelf. _____ finally comes to him, saying, "Sasha, do you want some blocks?" Sasha nods enthusiastically. _____ brings Sasha an armful of unit blocks.

What is your active-learning approach to the "I-Need-Some-Blocks" problem?

84

c) "I want to make a big, big, car," Raymond tells _____ at planning time. "Big enough to sit in."

"You'd better use the big blocks then," _____ responds, "and build them around you."

"What about a steering wheel?" Raymond asks.

"Use one of the big round Tinkertoys," _____ advises.

What is your active-learning approach to the "How-to-Make-a-Sit-in-Car" problem?

d) Brenda is so upset that she's hitting the workbench as hard as she can with her saw.

"What's the matter?" _____ asks, taking Brenda's saw in one hand and holding Brenda with the other.

"This wiggly board won't stay still so I can't saw it," Brenda shouts in frustration.

"Well, here," _____ consoles, "I'll put the board in the vice for you so it will stay still." _____ fits the board into the vice and tightens the clamp. "There, now you can saw."

Give your active-learning approach to the "Wiggly-Board" problem.

e) It's small-group time, and since a number of graduate students are observing your classroom every chair is being used, leaving Timmy with nothing to sit on. "Teacher, there's no chair for me," Timmy announces.

"Well, go get one of the big hollow blocks," _____ replies. "You can turn it on its end and use that for your chair today, Tim."

Give your active-learning approach to the "No-Chair-for-Me" problem.

f) Clarice is very excited because she has brought a bag of walnuts for snack time. "My grandma growed these in California," she tells her group proudly. "She sended 'em in the mail."

"That's very nice," _____ replies, "but we can't eat them today because we don't have a nutcracker to crack open the hard shells with." Clarice's eyes fill with tears. "I'll bring in a nutcracker and we'll eat them tomorrow, okay?" _____ adds hastily. Clarice is only slightly mollified.

Give your active-learning approach to the "No-Nutcracker" problem.

g) "Hey, Teacher," a group of children approach _____ at outside time. "We're gonna make a big, big house with these great big boards."

"You mean with the railroad ties?" _____ asks.

"Yeh, we're all gonna help and then get inside."

"That's a good idea but the railroad ties are too heavy. Use the climber for your house instead."

"But. . ."

"The ties are too heavy. Use the climber," _____ repeats. The group disbands.

Give your active-learning approach to the "Too-Heavy-Ties" problem.

h) Review and discuss your solutions with your team members.

6. Making small-group times active

On pages 131-32 in **Young Children in Action,** two small-group times focusing on pineapples are described. The idea of this exercise is to figure out why one of these small-group times incorporates active learning whereas the other one doesn't.

a) Read through the description of the first small-group time and answer the following questions:

1. What *materials* are available for each child?

2. How are children *manipulating* materials?

3. What *choices* are children making?

4. What *words* are children using to describe their actions?

5. What *support* is the teacher giving to help children think about their actions?

b) Read through the description of the second small-group time and answer the following:

1. What *materials* are available for each child?

2. How are children *manipulating* materials?

3. What *choices* are children making?

4. What *words* are children using to describe their actions?

5. What *support* is the teacher giving to help children think about their actions?

c) Which small-group time incorporates active learning? What active-learning key experiences does it include?

d) Visit a preschool classroom. Observe a small-group time activity and answer the following questions:

1. What active-learning *key experiences* were incorporated?

2. What *materials* were available to each child?

3. How did children *manipulate* materials?

4. What *choices* did children make?

5. What *words* did children use to describe actions and observations?

6. What *support* was given by an adult?

7. What changes would you make in this activity to incorporate more active learning?

e) Review and discuss exercises *a-d* with your team members.

7. Making circle time active

Because circle time involves 15-20 preschoolers at once, action can easily turn into chaos, causing many adults to react with strictness in order to maintain control. Making circle time an active-learning experience will help adults avoid the two extremes of chaos and strictness. Do the following exercises with your team members:

a) You are planning a circle time that will help the children become more familiar with the names of the parts of their bodies and how various body parts can move. You decide to use the song, "The Hokey Pokey." ("You put your _____ in, you put your _____ out, you put your _____ in and you shake it all about. You do the hokey pokey and you turn yourself around. That's what it's all about.") For materials, each child will use his or her own body.

1. How will you build into this activity *choices* for each child?

2. How will children be able to describe their actions/observations in their own *words*? What if a child uses the wrong name for a body part?

3. How will you provide *support* and help children think about what they're doing? What if a child moves a body part but can't name it?

b) Since one of the children's favorite stories is _____ (fill in a children's book or story with which you are very familiar), you are planning a circle time in which the children act out this story.

1. The characters in the story are the following:

2. Since in the story there are only _____ characters and there are 15 children, some of the children will play the following parts (of additional animals, people, or objects appropriate to the story):

3. What *materials* will be available?

4. What *choices* will children make?

5. What will be the opportunities for children to use their own *words*?

6. What *support* will be given by adults? (Consider how this play will be organized, how it will get started, how it will end.)

c) Pick out a large-group activity you have done with preschoolers. Evaluate it in terms of active learning.

   1. What *materials* were available to each child?

   2. How did children *manipulate* these materials?

   3. What *choices* did children make?

   4. What *words* did children use to describe their actions?

   5. How did you *support* the children to enhance their thinking processes?

6. How would you change this activity if you were to do it again?

8. Active learning: Transforming troublemakers

In many situations, preschoolers who are "causing trouble"—fooling, bothering, hitting, disrupting—are doing so because they haven't anything else to do at the moment. There are two ways of looking at misbehavior. You can look at the *child* and think, "Troy is having a bad day today," or "Troy has a very short attention span," or "I wish Troy would stay home for a few days," or "Troy has a mean streak in him." Such statements about a child may help you rationalize his misbehavior, but they don't serve you to improve it.

Alternatively, you can look at the *activity* the child is supposed to be attending to and ask yourself such questions as, "Is this activity interesting to Troy? Are there materials he can use, choices he can make, opportunities for him to talk about what he's doing?" A change in the activity can cause a change in behavior. Generally, children who are actively involved are caught up in what they are doing and have little interest in or reason for causing trouble.

The following exercises describe troublesome situations in which changing the activity, to make it more active, could re-channel the troublemakers' energies. As you change the activity, remember to consider *materials, manipulation, choices, words,* and *support.*

a) At small-group time, _____ is holding up construction paper shapes, asking each child in turn to name the shape and color. Elise is very good at this and often calls out the answers before the child whose turn it is has a chance to speak. Troy is poking Mike under the table. When _____ asks him to put his hands on the table, he does so only to begin tipping back on his chair until he tips over.

Describe how you would change this small-group activity, retaining its focus on shapes and colors but making it an active-learning experience that would engage both Elise and Troy.

b) Jamison is very good at zipping, snapping, and tying and consequently is always the first person ready for outside time. Today, while he's waiting for everyone else, he's swinging on the door, letting in the cold air and making a racket. Finally, _____ tells Jamison to go sit in the quiet area until everyone else is ready. This angers Jamison so he dumps out all the puzzles. By the time he finally gets them all picked up, outside time is over.

    Describe an alternative way of dealing with Jamison's ability that would involve him in helping others take care of their own needs.

c) Your preschool class is visiting the neighborhood fire department. While a fireman tells the children how many feet of hose the hose truck carries, how much water the pumper truck pumps per minute, and other facts and figures, Corey begins to pull Denise's hair. Denise starts to cry, and _____ moves next to Corey holding both his hands. Corey tries to climb up _____ who finally takes him outside until the visit is over.

    Describe possibilities you would discuss with the fire station personnel that would make a future fire station field trip more active and thus more engaging for preschool children.

d) Describe a difficult situation you have encountered with a child, either in a preschool classroom or elsewhere.

e) In light of what you know about active learning, describe how you would handle the same situation again.

f) Review and discuss exercises *a-e* with your team members.

9. Supporting active learning

Today during work time as you watched the children in the block area, you saw the following:

Marketta was heaping up the small, colored blocks, then smoothing out the heaps, sometimes putting some of the red blocks together in one part of her collection. She also seemed to be feeling the blocks by rubbing them against her cheek and the back of her hand.

Mike was building towers and knocking them over. As one of his towers toppled, he seemed to notice that the cylindrical blocks rolled, so he tried rolling other round blocks as well as some of the rectangular ones.

Clarice was filling two dump trucks with blocks, carefully seeing which blocks fit into which truck. She also figured out how to make truck beds go up and down.

Sasha also had a small dump truck and three of four small blocks, which he repeatedly banged together, dumped into the truck, and dumped out again.

Discuss these observations with your team members. List the active-learning key experiences that occurred, ways to talk with these children about what they were doing, ways to encourage them to talk about what they were doing, and ways to extend their activities (by adding similar but new materials, for example, or by making suggestions of similar things they might try).

Child	Key Experiences Observed	Ways to Encourage Child to Talk About Activity	Ways to Extend Activity
Marketta			
Mike			
Clarice			
Sasha			

10. Observing active learning in a preschool classroom

Turn to the active-learning checklist on pages 304-5 in **Young Children in Action.** Spend a day in a preschool classroom looking for the items in the checklist and checking off the ones you find.

a) What are this classroom's greatest strengths in providing active learning for preschool children?

b) If this were your classroom, what changes would you make to incorporate more active learning?

11. Active-learning issues to ponder

a) What is something you really know about? How and over what period of time did you acquire this knowledge?

b) Looking back over all your schooling, which teachers do you consider outstanding? Why?

c) After the preschool years, is active learning still important? Why or why not?

d) You are setting up a nutrition and preschool center in a third-world country where, because of lack of resources, children are malnourished and passive. What impact will active learning have on them?

e) How does active learning relate to on-the-job training, apprenticeship, "the school of hard knocks," and the adage, "Experience is the best teacher"?

f) Is active learning in conflict with contemplation? Why or why not?

12. Active-learning projects

a) Return to exercise 7a in Chapter 3. With your team members, review your class presentation. Consider materials for each participant, manipulation of materials, choices for participants, language from participants, and support from you. If any one of these active-learning elements was missing or needed improvement, redesign the activity. If possible, repeat the presentation. Ask participants to compare your two presentations.

b) Apprentice yourself to someone skilled in an area of interest to you. Keep a journal of your experiences.

c) Pick an area of interest you have always wanted to learn about. Obtain a "how to" manual and follow the directions. Record your experiences.

d) Take the most academic class you have ever attended and plan how you would present a portion of the same material in an active-learning style.

e) In a preschool classroom, plan, carry out, and evaluate an active small-group time.

f) In a preschool, plan, carry out, and evaluate an active circle time.

Films and Publications

Films

Helping Children Make Choices and Decisions
[PS100] Set of five 16mm films; color, sound; 33 min total

Five short films that deal with aspects of the teacher's role in helping children make responsible, thoughtful, creative choices. The films were produced in several Head Start centers. Some of the dialogue is in Spanish.

1. A Good Classroom Is a Classroom Full of Choices
[PS101] (7 min)

Children should be able to choose what they're going to do, where they're going to work, what materials they'll use, who they'll work with. This film shows how teachers can structure the classroom environment and the children's activities to provide opportunities to make and carry out such critical choices.

2. Questions That Help Children Develop Their Ideas
[PS102] (7 min)

Strategies to help young children think through the process of bringing an idea to fruition—finding materials they can use, discovering solutions to problems, and expanding their original notions to take account of new information.

3. Exploring the Possibilities of the Room
[PS103] (7 min)

In order to make responsible and creative choices, children need to be aware of the alternatives available to them. Teachers demonstrate some ways to help young children explore the possibilities of the classroom—the many activities and materials to choose from and the many imaginative ways materials can be used.

4. Acknowledging Children's Choices and Decisions
[PS104] (6 min)

Some ways teachers can help children recognize when they've made a decision and followed it through. Children don't always talk about their choices; they don't always connect their actions to the choices they've made. A teacher can give a child support for his decisions by naming what the child has done, praising him, pointing out results, and helping him survey his activities.

5. Planning Activities That Include Choices
[PS105] (6 min)

Strategies for planning activities that allow children a degree of control, even when choices are limited, such as when the teacher is structuring an experience to meet certain goals or when routines and procedures are set (e.g., at lunch time or nap time).

Guidelines for Evaluating Activities
[PS150] Set of three 16mm films; black & white, sound; 58 min total; discussion guides included

These programs demonstrate alternative ways teachers can plan and carry out activities with a group of preschool children. Each program shows two contrasting styles of structuring and leading a group activity using similar materials but different teaching methods and goals. Useful for stimulating discussion of teaching styles and educational philosophies. An accompanying observation guide offers criteria by which to evaluate and revise classroom activities. Also included is a trainer's supplement that discusses the films in terms of the criteria in the guide and offers suggestions for revising the activities.

Contrasting Teaching Styles: Small-Group Time
[PS151] (8 min)

Contrasting Teaching Styles: Work Time, the Art Area
[PS152] (22 min)

Contrasting Teaching Styles: Circle Time
[PS153] (18 min)

Experiencing and Representing
[PS110] Set of four 16mm films; color, sound; 48 min total

These programs demonstrate the importance of direct experience and representational play and show how the preschool environment can promote both experience and representation. In each section two teachers discuss specific activities from their classroom and demonstrate a variety of teaching strategies.

Part I—A Way Children Learn
[PS111] (12 min)

Shows a variety of classroom activities in which children spontaneously represent things they've done or seen. Teachers discuss how children at different stages of intellectual development vary in their ability to hold details in mind and depict them in space and time. They also discuss the importance of representational play for later cognitive and academic development.

Part II—Starting with Direct Experience
[PS112] (12 min)

Some materials teachers can provide and techniques they can use to promote concrete experience in the preschool classroom as a basis for later representational activity.

Troubles and Triumphs at Home
[PS192] Set of four color filmstrips and cassettes; 70 min total

Let Them Do It
[PS195] (16 min)

This filmstrip discusses the importance of giving children household responsibilities and of encouraging them to do things for themselves—not just because they must develop self-help skills, but because of the important learning that takes place when young children stretch their mental and physical abilities. This presentation shows how a number of parents decided to stop "doing for" their children and began to encourage more independence. It also suggests how simple household adaptations and visual cues or reminders can make the difference for the child between being dependent on others and being able to do something independently.

Supporting Children's Intellectual & Physical Development
[PS161] 16mm film; black & white, sound; 59 min; discussion guide included

This film has eight un-narrated sections and shows several teachers conducting typical day care or preschool activities in a variety of teaching styles and situations. Designed for use in the training of teachers and curriculum assistants, the film shows the following scenes for discussion: a flashcard activity at sharing time; a "mystery bag" game; two children making fish in the art area and describing their activity to the teacher; a teacher using a hand puppet to discuss the day's weather; a teacher passing a pineapple around for the children to see, feel, smell, and eat; a teacher helping children make individual portions of playdough; children planting seeds and talking with a teacher about their "gardens"; a teacher reading a story about robins to the children and asking them questions about it. An accompanying training guide provides questions and learning activities for each section.

The Block Area
[PS191] Set of five color filmstrips and cassette tapes; 38.7 min total

1. Setting Up a Block Area *(7.5 min)*
How to set up a block area and arrange it so that it is well placed and logically organized; how to equip the area initially and then add materials as the children become more familiar with the area.

2. A Place to Explore New Materials *(6.5 min)*
How children explore materials by trying things out, using their senses, arranging objects, etc., and what a teacher can do to facilitate children's explorations.

Opportunities for Learning
[ID308] 16mm film; black & white, sound, (27 min)
This film is designed to stimulate discussion among parents and infant-caregivers. It illustrates the process of exploration and discovery that is characteristic of most one- and two-year-olds by following the activities of one child through a series of play situations. In order to learn from his environment, the child needs *materials* for playing and learning, *time* to try things out, *people* to help him and to have fun with, *freedom* to learn on his own. Each section of the film focuses on one of these elements and gives suggestions to parents on how they can provide opportunities for learning in the home.

Babies Like Attention
[ID309] 16mm film; black & white, sound (13 min)
Several clips from home visits chosen to stimulate discussion of the use of praise and encouragement with infants. Includes the spontaneous reactions of a group of mothers who watched themselves on videotape, interacting with their children. Each mother gives a summary of her views on praise and encouragement and suggests things she feels are important to remember when interacting with a child. A good introduction for parents to the home-visit situation.

A Special Kind of Mother
[ID310] 16mm film; black & white, sound; (15 min)
This film features and is narrated by a mother from High/Scope's Infant Videotaping Project. It focuses on some of the special skills a mother can learn. Interactions between this mother and her baby point up her ability to understand, interpret, and act upon her child's needs. Throughout the film she comments on her actions with the child and how she thought the baby felt at the time.

Learning Through Problems: A Baby's Point of View
[ID311] 16mm film; black & white; (10 min)
Often a problem that's easy for an adult, such as holding two rattles at the same time, is very difficult for a baby. This film asks viewers to observe events from the baby's point of view. It shows how complex reaching, holding, moving, and pulling can be for an infant and how babies' sensory-motor explorations and difficulties can be turned into learning experiences which are fun for both baby and parent.

Cans: Toys for Learning
[ID312] 16mm film; black & white; (17 min)
A practical demonstration of how a simple household object, a can, can be used as an educational toy. Infants are shown progressing from simple manipulation, to recognition of objects inside a can, to putting objects back inside the can. The film shows how activities can be made more complex once the infant becomes aware of the variety of the can's uses—for example, by adding a lid for the baby to remove and replace and by putting a hole in the lid through which the baby can drop objects. There are suggestions for using other household objects—e.g., pots and pans, Band-aid boxes—in a similar manner.

Responding to a Baby's Actions
[ID313] 16mm film; black & white; (24 min)
Babies have special ways of letting adults know their participation is wanted. Adults' responses can take many forms. Some of the possible adult responses are illustrated in this film: imitating the baby's sounds, exploring objects and toys with the baby, joining in a game the baby has started. Following a summary of these responses, three un-narrated examples of adult-child interactions are presented for use in group discussions, for which a discussion guide is included.

Your Baby's Day: A Time for Learning
[ID321] Color filmstrip/cassette; (12 min)
Demonstrates appropriate activities for adults which will enhance babies' development through routine activities such as feeding, changing, and bathing. The program is designed to make parents aware of their vital role in a baby's development at three important stages: newborn, four to eight months, and eight months to a year. Useful for parents-to-be, for high school and community college courses in child development, for training adults in day care centers. Realistic, supportive suggestions for adult-infant interactions. Print guide included.

Publications

Learning Through Sewing and Pattern Design
(#15) Author: S. Mainwaring; booklet (35 pages); 1976.
This unique description gives suggestions for establishing a sewing area in the classroom and how to make it a vital center for learning and cognitive development. Also included is a discussion of spatial and temporal relations inherent in sewing, and projects and problems typical of children in an elementary classroom. Ideal for use not only by teachers but also leaders of boys and girls in scouting, YMCA-YWCA, and other youth groups.

Children as Music Makers

(#17) Author: L. Ransom; booklet (78 pages); 1979.
The guide gives strategies for teachers to support classroom music activities by providing instruments, space, time, and encouragement. The author shows how children readily explore instruments and discover basic elements of music, how they learn to make music and write it down, thereby applying math and language skills in the process. Included are a wealth of classroom-tested ideas for small-group and large-group activities, descriptive examples of children's musical representations, a glossary, and lists of suggested books and supplies.

Teaching Movement and Dance

(#40) Author: Phyllis S. Weikart
Teachers will discover how to provide students of all ages with successful rhythmic movement experiences through the step-by-step, easy-to-follow sequence of actions and expressions presented in this book. The book also presents the theory behind the learning process for achieving rhythmic movement, thus giving teachers an in-depth understanding of *why* as well as *how* to teach movement and dance to all age groups and special populations. Teachers of movement and dance will welcome this book because of its down-to-earth perspective, its practical guidance and advice, and its sound theoretical base.

Write or call the High/Scope Foundation, 600 North River Street, Ypsilanti, MI 48197, (313) 485-2000 to obtain information on ordering these materials.

6/Language

Language—putting actions, experiences, thoughts, feelings into words—is part and parcel of active learning. Language keeps experience "on tap." Doing is not enough, but doing put into words transforms actions into understanding and turns events into information that can be recalled and used in other situations. Actions supply information, while language makes the information accessible. Preschoolers are busy putting actions into words.

1. Child study: Babies' language

By the time they reach preschool, children have already spent a good deal of their lives listening to and using language. Without any formal training, they have mastered the complexities of sentence structure, for example. They may say, "I go store," but they never say, "Store I go." As their parents talk, read, and sing to them, babies not only learn to use language through imitation but also discover the joys and intimacies of verbal communication. The idea of this exercise is to examine the beginnings of language and to see how it has developed by the time a child is three or four years old.

a) Find five children whom you can observe for 15-30 minutes each. They should be of the ages shown in the chart below. One should be your "child-study" child. As you observe each child note what sounds and/or words he or she makes, what or who seems to inspire or motivate these sounds/words, and what role you or another person plays in the "conversation."

Child	Sounds/Words	Motivators	Second Person's Role
(less than one-year-old) *Name:* *Age:*			
(one- to two-year-old) *Name:* *Age:*			

(two- to three-year-old) *Name:* *Age:*			
(three- to four-year-old) *Name:* *Age:*			
(four- to five-year-old) *Name:* *Age:*			

b) From the five children you observed, what conclusions can you draw about language development in young children?

c) Describe recollections of your own early language development.

2. Recognizing key experiences in language

It is one thing to read about children's language and the understanding it represents, and it is another thing to hear, recognize, and support children's key language experiences as they occur naturally in the classroom. Following are monologues and conversations from actual preschool classrooms. After reading each one, you will choose from the list below the key language experience(s) that most accurately describe(s) the conversation or monologue.

Key Experiences: Language

- Talking with others about personally meaningful experiences

- Describing objects, events, and relations

- Expressing feelings in words

- Having one's own spoken language written down and read back

- Having fun with language

---

a) "Hey, I'm gonna set next to you on the bus, okay Rickey?"
"Okay."
"I don't like them skeletons hangin' on the doors. They's scary and they's real mean."
"Oh, I ain't scared of them things. They just paper."
"I'm scared, I'm not wearing no mask on Halloween. No siree."
   Identify the key experience(s):

b) "What can you tell me about your picture, Cara?"
"Snow."
"Oh, this is snow. It looks like lots of snow."
"Pile." (Cara points to another part of the picture).
"This is a pile of snow or a pile of something else?"
"Something else."
"Oh, it's a pile of something else that's all different colors."
"Blanket."
"Oh, I see. This is a blanket made out of lots of colors and it's all piled up."
"Yep."
"Did somebody leave the blanket outside in the snow?"
"Nope. Dog chewed it."
"Oh, dear."
"All wet."
"Now the blanket is all wet."
"Yep, all wet."
   Identify the key experience(s).

c) "What would you like to say on your mom's Valentine card, Barrel?"
"A story."
"A story? Okay. You tell me what to write down, and I'll write it on your card for you."
"Okay."
"What happens first in your story?"
"The mom got toys for the boy. Her said, 'Do you want some toys?' He said, 'Yes, I want some!' Her buys all the toys. He got a Rough Rider and a Hopper Wheely Car and all the toys. 'Here's your card,' he said."
    Identify the key experience(s):

d) "Rebecca, Jeff would like to make a book. Can you tell him how you made yours?"
"Okay. Well, you take all the paper and put it together so it all fits together and you hit it up and down so it fits together. And then you staple it along the side so it will stay, and then you write your story in it."
    Identify the key experience(s).

e) "This is where the mom sits, and this is where the dad sits, and this is where the little boy sits, and baby's over here, and outside over here's the car for when they go to their grandma's house far, far away."
    Identify the key experience(s).

f) "Teacher, guess what! My dog got hurt all over his eyes an' we had to take him to the dog doctor's 'cause blood was all over his fur."
"That's too bad, Terry. Is your dog still at the doctor's?"
"Nope. We bringed him home 'cause the doctor sewed him all up. You can see thread stickin' right in his face."
"I'm glad your dog's getting better."
"How'd he get those cuts, Timmy?"
"My dad says he got into some 'coons. He tried to bite 'em. They scratched him with their claws."
    Identify the key experience(s).

g) "Look, see this cake, Teacher. I helped make it, and we can have it for snack 'cause it's my birthday today."

"Well, happy birthday, Joey."

"I'm so excited! Hey, Donna, today's my birthday and I'm five, this many." (Joey holds up five fingers.)

"It is exciting to have a birthday, Joey. Can you put your beautiful cake up on the shelf, then take your coat off and come back and make a plan?"

"Okay, but I don't know if I can wait, and at home I'm havin' another cake and lots of presents. I can't wait! Hey Tracey, wanna' see my cake? I'll give you some at snack time. I put on the frosting. . ."

   Identify the key experience(s).

h) "Hey, Teacher, my sister teached me this new song: Jump rope, jump rope, all the way to antelope."

   Identify the key experience(s).

i) "Truckity truck, stuckity stuck. Truckity truck, stuckity stuck."

   Identify the key experience(s).

3. Asking questions that help children think

One way adults can stimulate thought and language in preschool children is by asking questions that make children think. *Divergent* questions have more than one right answer. They encourage children to express their ideas, feelings, and predictions.

"What do you think would happen if. . ."

"What do you think is in this box?"

"How can we try to get the seeds out of our pumpkins?"

Thought-provoking questions have a right answer that is based on children's direct observations of materials they are using or experiences they are having. Thought-provoking questions encourage children to classify, seriate, use numbers, or observe the relationships of space or time.

"What did you do in the art area today?"

"How many red blocks are there in your tower?"

"Which one of your clay balls is the biggest?"

Minimal-response questions call for a "yes" or "no" answer.

"Is that a triangle?"

a) Decide whether each question below is divergent (D), thought-provoking (TP), or minimal-response (M). When you find a minimal-response question, rewrite it so that it is divergent or thought-provoking.

1. "I see you've got the cars out, Corey. Are you going to build a road?"   D TP M

2. "You know, Clarice was having some trouble today hanging up her painting because the drying line is too high. What are some things Clarice could try tomorrow if she has another picture to hang up?"   D TP M

3. "Brenda brought us a surprise for snack today and it's in this bag. What do you think it is?"   D TP M

4. "This morning we took a special trip to the fire station. What's the very first thing the fire chief showed us?"   D TP M

5. "Troy, you took Marketta's scissors and now she's crying because she doesn't have anything to cut with. What could you do to make her feel better?"   D TP M

6. "Sam, are you going to give that puzzle back to Sasha or not?"   D TP M

7. "My goodness, Mike. This is the most delicious bottle cap soup I've ever tasted! I'd like to know your recipe so I can make it myself sometime. How many bottle caps did you use?"   D TP M

8. "For small-group time today we have buttons, straws, macaroni, string, paper, and glue. What are some things you could do with these things?"   D TP M

9. "The monkeys stole the peddler's caps. If you were the peddler, how would you get them back?"   D TP M

10. "What a colorful picture, Timmy. Is it a rainbow?"   D TP M

11. "We're going to have fun making up rhymes today. What's a word
    that starts with *M* and rhymes with house?"   D TP M

12. "What a neat way to make a car, Elise. What are you going to put
    on it next?"   D TP M

13. "I know clean-up time is hard, but what do you think would
    happen if we played every day but we never cleaned up?"   D TP M

14. "Raymond, you put some of the animals in your barn and some out
    in the pasture. What's the same about all the animals you put in
    your barn?"   D TP M

b) Write three *divergent* questions.

c) Write three *thought-provoking* questions.

d) Review and discuss exercises *a-c* with your team members.

4. Supporting communication among children

Another major role for adults in a preschool classroom is to support and encourage children's efforts to talk, listen to, and learn from each other. Adults can use the following strategies:

```
                              Strategies

  •  Encouraging interaction and cooperation      •  Interpreting and delivering messages

  •  Referring one child's questions or           •  Encouraging active listening
     problems to another
```

a) Read through the following conversations taken from actual preschool classrooms and, for each one, decide which of the four strategies just listed is being used. There are some conversations in which adults miss an opportunity for supporting communication. In these conversations, rewrite the adult's part so that the adult supports the child-to-child communication. You may want to refer to pages 150-54 in **Young Children in Action.**

1. Adult: Did you hear what David said, Peter?
   Peter: What?
   Adult: Could you tell Peter what he might be able to do so his trees wouldn't fall down?
   David: You could use them on the floor, Peter.
       Which strategy is used?

2. Joannie: Mo, mo.
   Teacher: She's saying, "Move," Christi.
       Which strategy is used?

3. Laura: I wanna use the big Tinkertoys, too.
   Adult: Why don't you talk to Andy, see if you can work together?
   Laura: Hey Andy, wanna work together with those?
   Andy: Okay. We'll have to make it big for both of us.
       Which strategy is used?

4. Adult: Hey, Troy, Andy's trying to get his screw eye in. I wonder if you have some ideas on how he could do it.
       Which strategy is used?

5. Dan is pushing Contrell.
   Adult: Talk to him, Dan. Tell him what you want to do.
   Dan: Will you move so I can make these trucks go through?
       Which strategy is used?

6. Adult: Hey, Tom, you know the masks that you've been making? That's the kind Alvin
   wants. Could you help him make one?
   Tom: You want a green one, Alvin?
       Which strategy is used?

7. Contrell: What did Pookie bring in that cage?
   Adult: She brought her guinea pig.
   Contrell: Can I hold it?
   Adult: It might run away.
       Which strategy is used?

8. Adult: Tara, tell Shantell how she can put the wheels on.
   Tara: Put the wheels on here so. . .
   Adult: Look, Shantell, and listen to what Tara is telling you.
   Tara: . . . so they won't drag.
       Which strategy is used?

9. Tom: I want to do an idea and he (Mike) won't let me do it, an' I'm mad.
   Adult: I don't blame you. I think you have good ideas. Mike, didn't we talk about this? Other
   people have good ideas, too. Maybe you could work together and use both your ideas.
       Which strategy is used?

10. Liz: I wanna plane just like Maura's. How'd she make hers?
   Adult: Well, first she folded her paper in the middle like this. . .
       Which strategy is used?

b) Write a conversation using the students in your community-service classroom. Make it a conversation in which you *encourage interaction and cooperation* between Sam and Mike.

c) Write a conversation in which you *refer* Denise's *problem* to Timmy.

d) Write a conversation in which you *interpret* Sasha's "words" to Corey.

e) Write a conversation in which you *encourage* Brenda *to listen* to Raymond.

f) Review and discuss exercises *a-e* with your team members.

5. Stimulating conversations

Many young children have learned to negotiate without words. Family members and friends understand and respond to their shorthand system of looks and gestures. This nonverbal communication, though clever and efficient, is effective only for relatively simple expressions in sheltered surroundings. It is therefore important in classrooms to encourage and stimulate verbal conversations whenever possible.

Many opportunities for conversations between children arise every day in the preschool classroom. Suppose that you are in your classroom and spot the following situations:

a) Marketta and Denise are playing at the sand table. Marketta is filling up cups and turning them over for cakes while Denise is doing the same thing with muffin tins. Marketta brings over a pitcher full of water which she pours on top of some of her cakes. Denise holds out a can and, without a word, Marketta fills it up for her.

1. How would you join Marketta and Denise?

2. What would you do and say to get Marketta and Denise to talk with one another?

b) It's snack time. Your group is busy spreading celery sticks with peanut butter. Brenda is pulling the "strings" off her celery while Corey watches her, wide-eyed. No one says anything.

    Describe what you would do and say to get Brenda and Corey to talk to each other.

c) Clarice is sitting on the seesaw, looking at Sasha, who is standing next to Clarice, looking at her. It looks to you as if Clarice wanted someone to seesaw with her and that perhaps Sasha wanted to seesaw. Since neither one is saying anything, you step in.

1. How would you join Clarice and Sasha?

2. How would you help them talk to one another?

3. How would you try to help them continue talking once they both got on the seesaw?

d) It's recall time. Michelle is describing how she made her birdhouse in the construction area, but she's talking directly to you. The other children are quiet but don't appear to be paying much attention. Sam's playing with his sweatshirt zipper; Michelle's coloring her fingernails with a green magic marker; and so on.

Describe what you would do to open up Michelle's monologue so that it included other children.

e) Review and discuss exercises *a-d* with your team members.

6. Acknowledging children's choices and decisions

In a preschool classroom where children feel good about themselves and what they can do, it is not unusual to hear one child say to another, "That's a good idea" or, "I have an idea. We could . . ." When children hear adults acknowledging choices and decisions, they do it too.

Below are three conversations conducted in different styles, one of which acknowledges Lynnette's choices and decisions. Together with your team members, read the three conversations and then do exercises a-d.

Conversation A

Adult: Lynnette, what did you make?
Lynnette: A fish.
Adult: A fish! Are those his fins?
Lynnette: Yes.
Adult: What a good idea! What did you use to make your fish? What's this right here?
Lynnette: A balloon.
Adult: A balloon. And what's this over here? (points)
Lynnette: Some paper.
Adult: Okay. And what did you use to stick the paper on?
Lynnette: Some glue.
Adult: Some glue, you're right. And what's this I see right here, this stuff here? (pointing)
Lynnette: Sparkles.
Adult: Sparkles. Okay. Or glitter. I think that's a beautiful fish. Would you like to hang it up?

Conversation B

Adult: Lynnette, look what you made! What can you tell me about it?
Lynnette: It's a fish.
Adult: You made a fish out of your balloon. What a good idea! Tell me what some of the parts are on your fish.
Lynnette: These are paper—all different colors of paper, and this, this is glitter.
Adult: So you made the fish all different colors and glittery—so it's kind of shiny. What are these parts here?
Lynnette: Those are the eyes and this is the mouth and these are the scary parts.
Adult: So you used round pieces of paper to make eyes and the glitter to make it scary. Boy, it sure looks scary to me! Those were good ideas, Lynnette. Is there anything else you're going to add to your fish?

Conversation C

Adult: Oh, Lynnette! Look what you made! That's beautiful. Is it a face?
Lynnette: No. It's a fish!
Adult: Oh, a fish! Well, that's certainly a very nice fish. I think we should hang the fish up so everyone can see it.

   a) Decide which conversation best acknowledges Lynnette's choices and decisions, and
      underline the parts of the conversation that do.

117

b) List and analyze the kinds of questions the adult asked in the other two conversations—divergent, thought-provoking, or neither.

Question	Type

c) Compare Lynnette's contribution in the "acknowledging-style" conversation with her contributions in the other two conversations.

118

d) Describe why the "acknowledging-style" conversation is the best of the three conversations.

e) Find a preschool-aged child who is doing or making something. Talk with the child about what she or he is doing. Acknowledge the child's choices and decisions. As you talk, tape record yourself or have a team member act as a scribe. Afterwards, review your conversation; list your questions and analyze them; list your acknowledging statements.

Questions/Acknowledgments	Type of Question

f) How could you improve this conversation?

g) Find another child in another situation. Repeat your experiment. Record your findings.

Questions/Acknowledgments	Type of Question

h) How did you improve?

7. Taking dictation

For young children who cannot yet read or write, dictating stories provides an intimate connection with written words. Review pages 164-65 in **Young Children in Action**. Use your "child-study" child for the following dictation exercise:

a) Ask the child to tell you a story or to tell you about a recent experience. Write the dictated account in the space below. (Put carbon paper and another sheet of paper under this page to make a copy to give the child.)

Child's Name _____ **Date** _____

b) After you have left the child, note down the child's response to the dictating process, any questions you asked to nudge the story along, and recommendations to yourself for the next time you elicit a story from this child.

8. Reading aloud

Being read to is another way preschool children make the connection between written and spoken words. Although they can't yet read or write themselves, they begin to realize that words can be written down and read back the same way over and over again. Being read to also allows children to enjoy hearing language well used.

The following are some qualities to look for in selecting books to read aloud to preschoolers:

+ Rhyming Repetition (Rhy Rep)
  Words and phrases that appear predictably throughout the story, rather like a chorus or refrain. Children can learn and repeat them easily.

+ Language Well Used (LWU)
  Language that's pleasant and exciting to read aloud. Interesting, varied vocabulary. Sentences flow.

+ Consistent Logic (CL)
  Characters (human, animal, or vehicular) act and solve problems within a given coherent framework. In the *Babar* stories, for example, elephants consistently act like human beings and human beings accept elephants who act like people without batting an eyelash.

The following are some qualities to avoid in selecting books and stories to read aloud to preschoolers:

- Choppiness (Chop)
  Short, choppy, abrupt sentences that are hard to read aloud.

- Lackluster Language (LL)
  Limited vocabulary, unvaried sentence structure and length.

- Aimless Plot (AP)
  Things happen for no particular reason. Lack of resolution.

- Didacticism (D)
  Stories written solely to "educate" (be a dentist; don't litter; everything has a color).

a) Read the following selections from children's books. Circle the qualities that apply to each selection.

Selection	Qualities	
	+	-
Charles sat on the toy shop shelf. Day after day he sat all alone between the painted dolls. "I do not belong to anyone," thought Charles. "Nobody belongs to me." The shopkeeper was not unkind. He smiled as he dusted Charles off. "There now," he said, "that feels better, doesn't it?" "No," thought Charles, "that doesn't feel better. I wish I were a wild bear," thought Charles. But the shopkeeper went whistling on his way.	Rhy Rep LWU CL	Chop LL AP D
One day the Duchess sat up in the tower, She had listened to minstrels for many an hour. She was bored with embroidery, tired of talking, She hoped no one suggest that she venture out walking. So she sat in the tower and thought what she'd do While the girls were at school and Duke busy, too. Then, quickly, she sat up, a light in her eyes— "Why, I'll bake them a cake—what a lovely surprise!" So she raced down the turret, three steps at one leap, Cleared the help from the kitchen and said, "Don't you peep. You'll all be delighted, for I'm going to make A lively light luscious delectable cake."	Rhy Rep LWU CL	Chop LL AP D
There was a bib-bibbidy-rib-ribbidy *rip* as the wheels ricketed over rocks and ruts and tore loose from the wagon, flying their separate ways. Ebenezer somersaulted backward over the backboard, and Farmer Palmer kissed the ground as the wagon shot over him.	Rhy Rep LWU CL	Chop LL AP D
The wolverine is a weak-sighted animal that lives in the wilds of North America. The wolverine is something of a bandit. It waits until a family leaves the house. Then it steals in and eats all the food it can find. The wolverine also steals bait from hunters' traps.	Rhy Rep LWU CL	Chop LL AP D
The music was furnished mostly by the Musical Soup Eaters. They marched with big bowls of soup in front of them and big spoons for eating the soup. They whistled and chuzzled and snozzled the soup, and the noise they made could be heard far up at the head of the procession where the Spoon Lickers were marching. So they dipped their soup and looked around and dipped their soup again.	Rhy Rep LWU CL	Chop LL AP D

On a bimulous night, the sky is like lace.
Do you know how it looks when it's
    bimulous and the sky is like lace?
It doesn't happen often, but when it does—
    KA-BOOM!
—and everything is strange-splendid and plum-purple.
	Rhy Rep
	LWU
	CL
		Chop
		LL
		AP
		D

Selections	Qualities	
	+	−
Dog. Big dog. Little dog. Big dogs and little dogs. Black and white dogs. "Hello!" "Hello!" "Do you like my hat?" "I do not" "Good-bye!" "Good-bye!"	Rhy Rep LWU CL	Chop LL AP D

b) Discuss exercise *a* with your team members. Decide which of the selections are from stories you would read aloud to preschool children.

c) Go to the library and select five books to read aloud to preschool children, based on the criteria just listed. List the books and describe why you chose them.

Book (Title/Author)	Why Selected

9. Encouraging language throughout the daily routine

The daily routine provides numerous opportunities for children to talk with one another about what they are planning, doing, remembering, observing, feeling, and enjoying. The following is a list of language opportunities that occur throughout the day. (They are lettered from A-N so you can refer to them by letter in doing exercises *a* and *b*.) Do these exercises together with your team members.

Opportunities for Child Language	Opportunities for Adult Support of Child Language
A Talking with others about personal experiences B Describing objects, events, and relations C Expressing feelings in words D Having spoken language written down and read back E Having fun with language: rhyming, making up and listening to stories, poems	F Asking questions that help children think G Encouraging interaction and cooperation H Referring one child's questions to another I Interpreting and delivering messages J Stimulating conversations K Encouraging active listening L Acknowledging children's choices and decisions M Taking dictation N Reading aloud

a) List three language opportunities that are available in planning time. For each opportunity, write a sample conversation. An example is given.

Language Opportunity	Sample Conversations
A	Mike: My log splitter's going to be like my dad's log splitter. His has a lever and he lets me push it. Screech, it goes, very loud. Then it rams 'em real hard.

125

b) List three language opportunities available in each of the other segments of the daily routine and give a sample conversation for each one you list.

Language Opportunities	Sample Conversations
(Work Time)	
(Clean-up Time)	
(Recall Time)	
(Snack Time)	

(Small-Group Time)	
(Circle Time)	
(Outside Time)	

10. Talking with children who don't talk

In every preschool classroom there are children who, for one reason or another, don't talk. They may be shy. They may be developmentally delayed. They may speak a different language. They may use a personal language comprehensible only to themselves and their families. However, it is vitally important for such children to be talked to by adults and other children. It is only by being intimately included in verbal exchanges and by hearing language that any person—infant, preschooler, adult—learns to use language.

Following are descriptions of four children in your preschool classroom who have specific language problems. Consider the strategies offered in Chapter 6 of **Young Children in Action**, as you read the descriptions. Do exercises a-d with your team members.

Although Sasha is a Down's Syndrome child and doesn't use any language, he has a very complex and effective system of grunts, noises, and gestures. Using this system, he's very much a part of whatever is going on in the classroom. During planning time he can indicate an area and objects he wants to work with and often plays quite cooperatively with other children who accommodate to his personal communication system. Because he is so adept at expressing himself without words both at school and at home, you feel that perhaps Sasha could talk but simply has no reason to. Therefore, you decide to plan some ways that would encourage him to use actual words in place of his gestures. At planning time, for example, you're going to try having him say after you the name of the area to which he points.

a) What are four other strategies you could try?

1.

2.

3.

4.

Denise never says a word in school. She's alert and aware of what is going on around her and can indicate what she'd like to do at planning time. She has no trouble comprehending language; she just doesn't use it. In talking with her parents, you are surprised to learn that at home she talks quite a bit.

b) What are four strategies you could try to encourage Denise to talk with you and other children in school?

1.

2.

3.

4.

Troy becomes frustrated very easily. He takes his frustration out by throwing things and knocking over other people's work and ends up feeling worse than he did to begin with. He rarely talks, even when things are going well for him. Outside, however, Troy is a different person. He is extremely well coordinated and can climb, throw, and catch better than anyone else. Other children look to him for help and assistance which he gives. Outside he also talks freely with both children and adults about what he's doing and things he does at home with his brothers and sisters.

    c) What are four strategies you could try to help Troy talk and be as successful in the classroom as he is outside?

        1.

        2.

        3.

        4.

Juanita, a four-year-old, has just joined your preschool classroom. Her parents come from Puerto Rico and only her father speaks some English. Juanita is very verbal, alert, and able. She speaks well in Spanish, but no other person in the classroom can speak Spanish.

    d) What are four strategies you could try with Juanita so she could communicate verbally with other children and adults?

        1.

        2.

        3.

        4.

11. Observing children's language in a preschool classroom

Turn to the language checklist on pages 305-8 in **Young Children in Action**. Spend a day in a preschool classroom looking for the items on the checklist and checking off the ones you find.

a) Describe this classroom's greatest strengths in providing opportunities for language between children.

b) If this were your classroom, describe the changes you would make to provide more opportunities for language between children.

12. Child study: Language

Child's Name: _____   Date: _____

Child's Age: _____   Location: _____

a) Watch and listen to _____. Make notes about how, to what extent, about what, and to whom _____ is talking.

b) Considering your observations, what language strategies will you use for joining _____?

c) What happened when you tried out these strategies?

d) What did you learn about the way _____ uses language?

13. Language issues to ponder

a) What is the relationship between the language children use and a well-organized classroom?

b) What is the relationship between children's actions and their language?

c) How would you take dictation from a child whose language you do not understand?

d) Suppose you were blind and you were looking for a preschool in which to enroll your child. As you visited potential classrooms, what would you listen for?

e) Children used to be raised according to the belief that children should be seen but not heard. How might the practice of such a belief affect children's language development?

14. Language projects

a) Visit a preschool classroom blindfolded. Considering just what you could hear, evaluate the classroom using the active-learning and language checklists in **Young Children in Action,** pages 304-8.

b) Watch a children's television show. How would you evaluate it with regard to providing key language experiences for children?

c) Tape record yourself in a preschool classroom for at least 30 minutes. As you listen to the tape, answer the following:

1. What questions did you ask?

2. What ways did you support communication among children (by encouraging interaction, referring questions to children, delivering messages, encouraging active listening)?

3. Give examples of how you acknowledged children's choices and decisions.

4. Give examples of other ways you supported children's language.

5. Who talks more often on your tape, you or the children? Why?

6. What are your strengths in providing language opportunities for children?

7. What do you need to work on in providing language opportunities for children?

d) Make a collection of preschool children's dictated stories, letters, and ideas. Make carbon copies for the children. Make notes on the children's responses to the process and on your role in eliciting the dictation.

Films and Publications

Films

Supporting Communication Among Preschoolers
[PS145] 16mm film; black & white, sound; 3 reels, 78 min total
This seven-part film deals with the cognitive, social, and linguistic aspects of communication and illustrates a wide variety of teaching strategies for stimulating communication among preschoolers. Parts I and II are narrated films. Parts III-VI illustrate teaching strategies and show unnarrated classroom episodes which viewers are asked to analyze; Part VII is a question-answer format with breaks for discussion.

Part I—An Important Opportunity
Examples of verbal communication in the classroom; the ways children use language and the benefits they gain from it.

Part II—Opportunities in the Classroom
How the daily routine can provide children with opportunities to communicate with one another. How teachers can support children as givers and receivers of information.

Part III—Encouraging Interactions and Cooperation
A presentation of teaching strategies to promote interaction and cooperation among children.

Part IV—Referring One Child's Questions or Problems to Another
Often children can help each other with problems that arise in the course of their activities. In asking and answering questions and helping each other to solve problems, they use language in important and meaningful ways. This film shows what teachers can do to encourage this type of interaction.

Part V—Interpreting or "Delivering" Messages
Sometimes a teacher needs to be a "go between" for children, helping one child understand what another is trying to say, helping the other to find ways to say what he means. Often the teacher may have to "deliver" messages that weren't received or acknowledged. This film illustrates several such situations.

Part VI—Encouraging Active Listening
Ways in which teachers can help children listen to, think about, and act upon each other's statements, questions, or suggestions.

Part VII—Examples for Discussion

Helping Children Make Choices and Decisions
[PS100] Set of five 16mm films; color, sound; 33 min total
Five short films that deal with aspects of the teacher's role in helping children make responsible, thoughtful, creative choices. The films were produced in several Head Start centers. Some of the dialogue is in Spanish.

2. Questions That Help Children Develop Their Ideas
[PS102] (7 min)
Strategies to help young children think through the process of bringing an idea to fruition—finding materials they can use, discovering solutions to problems, and expanding their original notions to take account of new information.

4. Acknowledging Children's Choices and Decisions
[PS104] (6 min)
Some ways teachers can help children recognize when they've made a decision and followed it through. Children don't always talk about their choices; they don't always connect their actions to the choices they've made. A teacher can give a child support for his decisions by naming what the child has done, praising him, pointing out results, and helping him survey his activities.

Experiencing and Representing
Set of four 16mm films; color, sound, 48 min total
These programs demonstrate the importance of direct experience and representational play and show how the preschool environment can promote both experience and representation. In each section two teachers discuss specific activities from their classroom and demonstrate a variety of teaching strategies.

Part I—A Way Children Learn [PS111] (12 min)
Shows a variety of classroom activities in which children spontaneously represent things they've done or seen. Teachers discuss how children at different stages of intellectual development vary in their ability to hold details in mind and depict them in space and time. They also discuss the importance of representational play for later cognitive development.

Part II—Starting with Direct Experience [PS112] (12 min)
Some materials teachers can provide and techniques they can use to promote concrete experience in the preschool classroom as a basis for later representational activity.

Part III—From Direct Experience to Representation
[PS131] (8 min)
Teaching strategies to help children represent their experiences: sequencing activities from the concrete to the abstract; structuring the classroom in a nondirective way to encourage children to represent ideas and experiences in a variety of media.

Part IV—Strategies for Supporting Representational Activity
[PS114] (16 min)
Teaching strategies that encourage children to add detail and complexity to their representations; shows the process of taking dictation from the child to stimulate verbal representation and to help the child learn that writing is a way of representing spoken language.

Let Them Say It [PS196] (18 min)
Many parents are concerned about their child's language development but are unsure of their abilities to support their child's language learning at home. This filmstrip describes how language can be a natural part of any activity and shows how parents can incorporate verbal (or sign) communication into such common daily activities as bathing, cooking, dressing, cleaning, etc. The filmstrip also suggests several general techniques for stimulating language usage such as: asking children to give instructions or directions, reading books in ways that stimulate conversation, and recording the child's language, stories, and experiences and then reading these back.

Publications

Writing and Reading *(#6)*
Author: O. B. Hsu; booklet (40 pages); 1977

The guide contains a plan for developing writing and reading abilities in children based on the following premises: 1) that writing and reading are best learned together; 2) that the child's initiation into literacy is a matter of discovering the connection between spoken and written language; 3) that the child discovers this connection best when personal experiences are the basis for the first attempts at writing and reading. Classroom writing activities can include dictating, tracing, copying, and eventually writing independently about the child's personal experiences. Reading begins with the child's own writing and subsequently includes writings by friends and printed materials. Strategies for extending children's stories and encouraging reading comprehension are also given. The appendices have detailed progressions of writing and reading abilities in relation to Piaget's developmental stages, as well as criteria for evaluating quality and content in children's stories.

Write or call the High/Scope Foundation, 600 North River Street, Ypsilanti, MI 48197, (313) 485-2000 to obtain information on ordering these materials.

7/ Experiencing & representing

Learning starts with action. Experience, as the old saying goes, is the best teacher. But for experiences to teach, they must be remembered. Representation helps people remember what they know. Language—putting experiences into words—is one way of representing and thus remembering. Painting, drawing, modeling, and role playing are other more tactile, three-dimensional ways of representing and remembering. Doing teaches, while representing fixes and holds the lesson somewhere in mind.

1. Child study: Observing the development of representation

Children represent their experiences in widely varying degrees of complexity and abstraction, depending on their age, level of development, and life experiences. Infants, for example, explore objects with their mouths, eyes, ears, hands, and noses, but they are also very active imitators. Young preschool children make very simple drawings whereas older preschoolers include more details in their drawings. The idea of this exercise is to watch a variety of children represent in a variety of ways.

a) Find five children of different ages whom you can work with and watch for 15-30 minutes. They should be of the ages shown in the chart on the following page. One of the children should be your "child-study" child.

Present each child with the following items: a cooking pan, a spoon, six small blocks, a magazine picture of a person, a doll, crayons, and drawing paper.

As each child plays with these materials fill in the chart with specific examples. You won't be able to fill in every square for every child. The youngest child, for example, may simply explore the objects by mouthing them (take necessary safety precautions), throwing them, and putting them in the pan. Make your notes as specific as possible.

Date: _____

Child	How Child Explored Objects	How Child Related Doll and Picture to Real People	How Child Role Played	How Child Made Models or Pictures	What Child Dictated
(six-month- to one-year-old) Name: Age:					
(one- to two-year-old) Name: Age:					
(two- to three-year-old) Name: Age:					
(three- to four-year old) Name: Age:					
(four- to five-year-old) Name: Age:					

b) Based on these five children, what conclusions can you draw about how children's ability to represent develops?

c) What do you remember about representations you made as a child? Do you or your parents still have any of your first drawings or models?

d) Share your findings in exercises *a* and *b* with your team members.

2. Recognizing key experiences in experiencing and representing

Following are descriptions of classroom situations in your preschool. In exercises *a* through *i* you will decide which experiencing and representing key experience(s) each situation depicts.

Key Experiences: Experiencing and Representing

- Recognizing objects by sound, touch, taste, and smell

- Imitating actions and sounds

- Relating models, photographs, and pictures to real places and things

- Role playing

- Making models

- Making drawings and paintings

- Observing that spoken words can be written down and read back

a) Lynnette, Mike, and Jamison have made a plan to dance to some records. After they put on a record with a good beat, Lynnette says, "I know how to shake my wrists." Mike and Jamison watch and try it too. Everyone takes turns making up steps and trying out everyone else's steps.
Identify the key experience(s).

b) You notice that Elise and Raymond have set up a grocery store in the house area. They have also used some boards from the block area to make a counter. Raymond asks you what you want to buy. "What's on sale?" you ask.
Identify the key experience(s).

c) Brenda calls you over to the art area to admire her painting. She tells you to get a pen so you can write down her story about her painting. You write down Brenda's story, then help her make a new plan.
Identify the key experience(s).

d) Just before outside time, while you are helping Clarice put on her overshoes, you hear the garbage truck making its daily stop across the street. You ask Clarice if she knows what is making that sound.
Identify the key experience(s).

e) At small-group time, you put out piles of shredded ribbons, sections of used computer cards, glue, and crayons. The children make collages with these materials. "See my playground," Lynnette announces excitedly.
Identify the key experience(s).

f) You notice that Corey seems to be stumped on where to go next with the camping van he is working on. You talk with Corey about what he has already done and discuss possible additions. Corey says he can't remember what else goes on a van, so together you go to look at a camping van parked outside. "Oh, I'm gonna put a ladder on my van and a tire in the back too," Corey decides.
Identify the key experience(s).

g) You are working with five children who plan to make soup. The children busy themselves washing, scraping, and cutting carrots, potatoes, and celery and putting pieces in the broth. Sasha seems to be confused about what goes in the pot and tosses in a plastic onion. You fish the intruder out and take a few minutes with Sasha to compare the real onion with the plastic onion. The children taste, touch, and smell both.
Identify the key experience(s).

h) During outside time, Marketta asks you to push her on a wooden taxi. You would like to involve Marketta in play with the other children so you "load up" the taxi with two other children besides Marketta. After a few rounds you stop pushing, saying that you're tired and someone else needs to push. Marketta volunteers.
"Brrruuummmmmm," she says. "I'm the motor."
Identify the key experience(s).

i) There's real vegetable soup for snack time. During small-group time, you have your group draw pictures of the different foods the children found in their soup. Sam makes his picture by tracing around various vegetable chunks. "Can't draw these," he says, indicating the celery ridges, " 'cause my paper's too wet!"
Identify the key experience(s).

j) Review and discuss exercises *a* through *i* with your team members.

3. Recognizing levels of abstraction

Representations range from very simple to very complex, from very realistic to very abstract. The simplest way to recall an orange, for example, is to place a real orange in front of you. If you ate the orange and left the peels and seeds, these real parts would serve to remind you of the whole. More abstract ways of recalling an orange would be a photograph, clay model, drawing, or painting of an orange. If you know how to read, the word "orange" can represent or bring to mind an orange even though the word itself bears no resemblance whatsoever to an orange.

Preschool children cannot read the word "orange," but they can explore oranges; cut them into salads; examine their seeds, peels, and sections; recognize pictures of oranges; and make models or drawings of oranges. Once they have done these things, the leap to deciphering the word "orange" at age six or seven is a natural one.

Your ability to recognize levels of abstraction helps you see what makes sense to children. It also helps you provide appropriate classroom materials. In exercises *a-d,* you will practice arranging things in order from the most realistic to the most abstract.

a) Arrange in order a photograph of children picking up shells on the beach, a book about shells, shell prints in the sand, a line drawing of a shell, shells the children gathered on the beach, a papier mâché shell.

Most realistic 1.

2.

3.

4.

5.

Most abstract 6.

b) Arrange in order a simple wooden firetruck, a detailed metal firetruck, *The Real Book of Firetrucks*, a firetruck bell, a firetruck made from a box with bottle cap wheels, a real fireman's boots and hat.

Most realistic 1.

2.

3.

4.

5.

Most abstract 6.

c) Arrange in order an eggshell collage, a chicken's egg, a plastic Easter egg, the book *Horton Hatches a Who*, egg-shaped Easter stickers, photographs of a chicken farm.

Most realistic 1.

2.

3.

4.

5.

Most abstract 6.

d) Arrange in order a blue silhouette of a cow, the book *Brown Cow Farm*, a reinforced cardboard cutout of a cow, a rubber model of a cow, a recording of cows mooing, a playdough cow.

Most realistic 1.

2.

3.

4.

5.

Most abstract 6.

e) Labels indicating where toys and materials go on shelves can be realistic or abstract. The most realistic label indicating where the blue crayons go, for example, would be an actual blue crayon taped to the shelf. The most abstract label for blue crayons would be a written sign—BLUE CRAYONS. For the items below, indicate how you would make four different kinds of labels varying in degrees of abstraction.

Items	Most Realistic Label	Less Realistic Label	More Abstract Label	Most Abstract Label
Cooking pans				
Scissors				
Dump trucks				
Puzzles				
Hammers				

f) Review and discuss exercises *a-e* with your teaching team.

4. Providing materials for experiencing and representing

If preschool children are to make a wide variety of representations, they need both real objects to work with and explore as well as materials with which to construct representations of objects. Consider materials from each area of a preschool classroom as you fill out the following chart. You may want to refer to the lists of classroom materials on pages 37-52 in **Young Children in Action.** Do this exercise with your team members.

Area	Real Objects for Exploring and Imitating	Models, Photos, and Pictures of Real Objects	Materials for Role Playing	Materials for Making Models, Paintings, and Drawings
Art Area				
Block Area				
House Area				
Quiet Area				

142

Music Area	Animal & Plant Area	Construction Area	Sand & Water Area

143

5. Starting with real objects

Many adults feel that they are teaching only when they are telling children something. Following this line of reasoning, imagine that you are in school and your teacher reads you the following story about "ballparks." Do this exercise with your team members. Choose one person to be the "teacher."

_____Ballparks Have Hit a New High*_____

We all know that ballparks are suddenly glamorous.

To tell the truth, the ballpark is not really a park at all, but a farm doing a very good imitation of a park. The ballpark clamp is a gumble like the tipa creep. The only difference is that for reasons known only to itself the ballpark has chosen to pippen overbeak instead of in the nippy ozo.

Shipped farm ballparks are clamped in soft, ploppy, or crumbly till in the maypole. The clamps stew quite quickly and trap mini yellow flappers. The curious part of the ballparks stewth begins when the flappers tilt and the remaining clips or "mits" cram themselves in the till in a process technically known as geocarpy. The ballpark develops at the end of those mits, the ships reaching their ruff phase well before the individual parks within cloister. In the piaget the clamp is ready for pestering. The clamps, ballparks and all, are simply tattooed by tracer and left to phed for a few days in the flack. The ballparks are then pished from the clips by tracers.

The ballpark heels generous stoves of "B" termitters, its lip is largely of the unpurpled variety, and three or four bushfuls remills the overgrown tempo mamford requirement. The ballpark is quite a park.

The origins of the ballpark are buried in history. The Headbands of Left and Right Free World were among the first to appreciate the park. Somehow the ballpark reached Crafica. There it became an important loop drop. The ballpark sled many shives during the shives' jerney to the Tied Terras. Its early days in this pantry were hued by this association. The prevailing term then was "sreboog."

The raw between the Terras gave the ballpark its big break. Leftyalls and even Keeney flukes began to leds screboog balls. Keeney's carried the ballpark clamor back Yonder and ballparks became famous as a chopper.

One sign of how fashionable the ballpark has become was an article in a well-known newspaper telling rakers how they could silter sreboog on shingledeckers.

a) Now that your teacher has read this story to you, answer the following questions to see how much you have learned:

1. The ballpark is not really a park, but is a _____.

2. Another name for ballparks is _____.

3. What is unusual about the ballpark's stewth and pippening?

4. What is "geocarpy"?

5. Although tracers usually tattoo the ballpark clamp, can rakers silter ballparks on shingledeckers? How do you know?

_____

*Created by Donna McClelland, Consultant, High/Scope Educational Research Foundation.

6. Which American president is most likely to have been familiar with ballparks, Abraham Lincoln, Jimmy Carter, or Ronald Reagan? Why?

b) Based on this experience, how do you think preschoolers would feel when asked, for example, to talk about or represent what they know about giraffes, after hearing a story about the habits and lives of giraffes?

c) If you wanted preschoolers to find out about giraffes, what sort of experience would you plan for them?

d) Turn to page 173 for "Ballpark Definitions." Translate the story into English. As you do so, remember that many words we use with young children are as unfamiliar and meaningless to them as "mamford" is to you.

e) Describe the experience you would plan for preschool children if you really wanted them to explore and learn about peanuts.

f) Once the children had the opportunity to explore and examine real peanuts, describe what kinds of materials you would provide so that they could represent what they knew about peanuts. How might they use these materials?

6. Child study: Imitation

Imitation—copying what other people do—is one of the very earliest ways children represent what they know.

a) Observe again the five children you used for exercise 1a on page 136. This time, as they play and interact with their families and friends, watch for imitation. (You may see the youngest child, for example, imitating sounds a parent makes or waving his or her arms just like an older sibling.) Record your observations in the following chart, starting with the youngest child and working up to the oldest child:

Child	How Child Was Imitating
Name: Age:	
Name: Age:	
Name: Age:	
Name: Age:	
Name: Age:	

b) From your observations, what conclusions can you draw about the development of imitation?

c) Together with your team members, plan how you would encourage preschool children to imitate at recall time.

d) Together with your team members, plan three circle-time games that would encourage children to imitate.

7. Starting with real experiences: Field trips

One way children can have experiences with real objects is by going on field trips—to construction sites, farms, grocery stores, botanical gardens. Recently in your preschool classroom, you've noticed that Timmy, Michelle, and Raymond have been building fire stations in the block area but seem confused about what to put in them other than firetrucks. Their play consists of going "rrrr" like a fire siren, driving the trucks out, around the block area, and back into the station again. In this exercise, you and your team members plan a field trip to the local fire station.

a) First you call the fire station, set a date and time, and talk about what the children could see and do at the fire station. During the course of the conversation, the following possible activities at the fire station are mentioned. Check the ones most appropriate to preschool children.

   ☐ Hearing about how many gallons of water each hose carries per minute

   ☐ Holding a fire hose; seeing how many hands will fit on the nozzle

   ☐ Ringing the firetruck bell

   ☐ Seeing a map locating all the fire alarm boxes in town that are wired into the fire station

   ☐ Seeing the firemen raise the ladder on the firetruck

   ☐ Watching a fireman slide down the pole

   ☐ Hearing about the medical qualifications of the rescue truck drivers

   ☐ Looking inside the rescue truck

   ☐ Seeing the living quarters of the firemen—beds, stove, refrigerator

   ☐ Hearing about how many pounds of hamburger the firemen consume in a week

   ☐ Trying on fire boots, hats, coats

   ☐ Hearing about the temperatures the fire boots, hats, and coats can withstand

   ☐ Hearing about how chemicals are used to put out fires

   ☐ Seeing photographs of the firemen rescuing a kitten from a tree

149

b) Next you talk about what you might bring back with you from the fire station to the classroom.

    1.   List things you could bring back from the fire station that children could include in their play.

    2.   List Polaroid photographs you could take to help children recall their visit.

c) You have just completed a successful trip to the fire station. The children have seen and done everything you had hoped they would. You've been able to take Polaroid photographs and bring back the things you listed. Now you are planning follow-up activities for the classroom. Building on the children's experiences, the photos, and the things you brought back, describe how you would help the children represent their trip to the fire station. Do this by filling out as much of the following chart as possible:

	Imitating and Role Playing	Relating Photos to Real Things	Making Models	Making Drawings & Paintings	Dictating
Work Time					
Small-Group Time					
Outside Time					
Circle Time					

8. Role play

Another way preschool children represent what they know is by taking on roles and pretending to be someone else. Read through the following description of a "store" role-play situation you observed at your preschool center.

"Here, I'm the money man, okay Timmy. I take the money. Here, you put all these things on the shelf so's the people can buy 'em."

"Is this a grocery store, Raymond?"

"Yep. This is a grocery store. Here, put these on the shelf."

"What about the money?"

"I'll get the money. Be right back."

Raymond goes to the art area and hurriedly cuts some green construction paper into rectangles while Timmy puts cans, egg cartons, milk cartons, and plastic fruit on store shelves made from blocks.

"Where you gonna put the money?" Timmy asks when Raymond returns.

"This big block. It's my register. Brrring, Brrring, Brrring. That opens it up," Raymond says punching "keys" on his "register."

"Well, money man, hope some people come to our store."

Brenda, Elise, and Jamison come over from the house area. Brenda, carrying a big purse and sporting a broad-brimmed straw hat and high heels, has her two children in tow, Jamison with a bottle and Elise carrying a teddy bear.

"Mamma, Mamma, buy candy. We want candy."

"No sir, you hush. That's bad for your teeth all that sticky sweet. Yuck!"

"But, Mamma, we wants some."

"You want a spanking? Now you go and get some food and eggs. Go on, now."

Timmy offers the two children a bag and together the three empty the store shelf into it.

"How much I owe you?" Brenda asks Raymond.

"That be $11. You got $11?"

"One, two, three," Brenda counts the buttons she has in her purse. "Nope, only $6."

"Okay, gimme $6. You want a sucker?" he asks the children and hands them each a Tinkertoy lollipop which they "lick" all the way "home."

"We home," Mamma announces. "Open the door. I've got the groceries." Elise opens a pretend door. They file through it one after another and shut it carefully behind them.

After each role-play element listed in the following chart, give as many examples as you can find in the "store" situation.

Element	Examples
Pretending to be someone else	

Element	Examples
Sharing the pretend role with others	
Using one object to stand for another	
Using actions and sounds as substitutes for real actions and sounds	
Using words to represent a make-believe situation or setting	
Talking to others within the context of the role-play situation	

9. Child study: Role play

Visit a preschool classroom, play group, cooperative nursery, or any other group of young children who play together. As you watch the children, look for the role-play elements. Give specific examples of what you see.

_____Role-Play Observation Guide_____

Place: _____   **Date:** _____

Children Observed   **Names:** _____   **Ages:** _____

_____

_____

_____

_____

Element	Examples
Pretending to be someone else	
Sharing the pretend role with others	
Using one object to stand for another	

Element	Examples
Using actions and sounds as substitutes for the real action or sounds	
Using words to represent a make-believe situation or setting	
Talking to others within the context of the role-play situation	

10. Recognizing experiences children will want to represent

A mother took her four-year-old son to see the movie *Black Beauty* because he liked animals. When it was over, he couldn't wait to tell his dad. "Dad, guess what! We sat in seats that go up and down and then got me some popcorn, and it got real dark. Some kids talked real loud, and the man had to come over and make 'em be quiet!"

"What was the movie about?" his dad asked.

"A horse," the son replied.

"What part did you like the best?"

"When the lights went off and we ate popcorn!"

Although his mother probably thought she was providing her little boy with the opportunity to see a good movie, what the little boy actually enjoyed was the experience of being in a movie theater. The next day after preschool he reported to his mom that "Me and Bennie made a movie theater in the block area, and tomorrow Mrs. Brickman is gonna help us make real popcorn!"

As you read through the following experiences, decide whether or not each experience is one a child would want to represent and why.

155

a) Tommy lives on a farm. Every night after supper, Tommy helps his dad feed the cows. First he helps his dad hitch a wagon to the tractor. Then he rides the wagon to the barn where he and his dad load the wagon with hay for the cows. Tommy climbs as high as he dares on the hay bales for the ride home, jumps down to open the pasture gate, closes it behind the tractor and wagon, and finally helps his dad pitch the bales into the outdoor feeder.

Explain why Tommy probably would or would not want to represent this cow-feeding experience.

b) A local policeman comes into Mrs. Rugby's day care center to talk about safety. All the children sit at his feet as he tells them about safety. "Now what do you do when you come to a corner?" he asks the children.

"Hold your mommy's hand," one little girl volunteers.

"That's right," the policeman says, "but first you stop, look, and listen. Can you say that?" After getting the children to repeat "Stop, look, and listen," he goes on to talk about the importance of wearing seat belts, not playing with matches, and not accepting rides or food from strangers. After finishing his talk, he gives each child a safety certificate that lists all the rules he has talked about on the back.

Explain why the children probably would or would not want to represent this safety lesson experience.

c) During outside time a group of parents came to help with a playground clean-up project. While Bobby's mom wielded the clippers, Bobby and three other children hauled branches away to the dumpster. "Look at me, I've got a long, long, heavy branch," said Gene.

"Leaves, leaves, look at all the leaves," Angela chanted brushing her face with a branch.

"I can carry lots and lots, " announced Bobby carrying five branches at a time. "Look at the big, big pile. It's bigger than my mom."

Linda, Sharon, and Sharon's mom were raking. "My rake's stuck again. It's teeth dig too far down," said Linda as she untangled her rake. "This grass needs a haircut. It's too long." So saying, Linda abandoned her rake for a pair of scissors.

"Look, there's bugs in this grass, way down by the dirt." Linda and Sharon's mom gathered around to examine the bugs Sharon had discovered.

Explain why the children probably would or would not want to represent this playground clean-up experience.

d) At Mrs. Atwood's table, children are making cream cheese and jelly sandwiches. Each child has a paper plate, a plastic knife, two slices of bread, a small paper cup of cream cheese, and one of jelly. "This breaks up the bread," says Eddie as he attempts to spread his cream cheese.

"This sure is funny looking—bumpy with spots."

"Ouch, my knife's sharp."

The sandwiches the children make are unique but thoroughly edible!

Explain why the children probably would or would not want to represent this sandwich-making experience.

e) Mrs. Bassfin is teaching a group of preschoolers how to tell time. She is holding a big cardboard clock face and turning the hands around to different "o'clocks." "Now when the big hand is here and the little hand is here, what time is it?" she asks.

"Time to clean up," Joshua volunteers.

"No," Mrs. Bassfin answers, "it's ten o'clock because the little hand is on the ten. Now what time is it?" she asks moving the little hand to the 11.

"Ten o'clock," shouts Andrew.

"No, it was ten o'clock last time."

"I think it's time for snack," suggests Margaret.

"No, not yet. Where's the little hand, Margaret?"

"Right there."

"On the what?"

"On the clock."

"No, it's on the number 11 so it's eleven o'clock. You say it, Margaret."

"Eleven o'clock. Now can we have snack?"

Explain why Joshua, Andrew, and Margaret probably would or would not want to represent this time-telling experience.

f) Go back to the situations you decided the children probably would not want to represent. Describe below how you could alter each experience to make it one children would want to represent.

11. Representing throughout the day

a) Reread the classroom observations in Figure 1 on pages 54-59 of this study guide. Write down all the examples of representations that occurred throughout the day described. Discuss your findings with your team members.

	Realistic Representations	More Abstract Representations	Most Abstract Representations
Outdoor Time			
Circle Time			
Small-Group Time			
Recall Time			
Clean-up Time			
Work Time			
Planning Time			

b) During what time(s) of day did the widest variety of representation occur? Why?

c) When did the least representation occur? Why?

d) Recall time enables children to represent by talking about, describing, and sharing what they've done during work time. For Denise and Sasha, what is the value of recall time in terms of representation?

e) You want to find out to what extent each child in your classroom is able to represent using crayons and paper. During what time(s) of day would you attempt to find out? How?

f) A friend of yours asks you to observe the preschoolers in her classroom to see how they represent. Due to your busy schedule, you can only spend one time period in her classroom to do this. Which time period would you spend? Why?

12. Classroom situations: What would you do if . . .

Do the following exercises with your team members:

a) Raymond and Jamison are playing Batman by running back and forth across the room singing the Batman song. Since this is disrupting just about everyone else, you pull Raymond and Jamison aside. What suggestions do you make that encourage them to continue their Batman play in a less disruptive manner? How else could they represent Batman?

b) Michelle comes to planning time with a post card of a *tyrannosaurus* from the natural history museum she visited with her family. "I want to make a dinosaur like this one, Teacher," she says. When you ask her what materials she would need, she has no idea. Describe three suggestions you might make, involving three different types of materials, to help Michelle get her dinosaur underway.

c) Troy has made a road for his car out of blocks and contented himself for several minutes pushing the car back and forth repeating "rum-rum-rum." When he cannot think of anything more to do, he begins running his car into other children's structures. When you join him, what do you suggest to redirect his energies back to his road and to extend that activity?

d) Whenever Denise goes to the block area, she decides to build a house. After making a very simple structure (no doors, windows, or separate rooms), she sits back, apparently feeling that she has finished, and just watches the other children in the area. When you join her today, what three suggestions do you make to help her elaborate her house?

e) Sam comes running up to you with an airplane he has just finished at the workbench. He is obviously very proud of it, and asks you to look at it. Describe three different ways you could respond that would involve representation.

f) Lynnette brings her pet goldfish to school. She is anxious to show it and talk about it with the other children. What do you suggest?

g) Corey is very proud of his elaborate block tower. At clean-up time, he does not want to take it down. What three alternatives do you offer him?

h) Every time Brenda draws a picture using crayons, she draws a person. Describe three ways you might attempt to help her expand her drawings.

i) Every time Timmy plays "ambulance driver," he jumps into his "ambulance," makes a siren noise, "fixes" a "wounded" person, and drives off. After talking with your teaching team, you decide on three possible ways to extend Timmy's ambulance play. Describe them.

j) It's small-group time. You have provided each child with colored paper, scissors, and paste. Your goal is to have each child use these materials to represent the playground outside. Even though you explain what you want them to do, the children start right in cutting fringes and strips and loading them down with paste. Should you try to get them to change their activity to meet your goal? Why or why not? By cutting fringes and pasting, what are these children telling you about their familiarity with scissors and paste? What would you plan to do with them tomorrow at small-group time?

k) Since you've just gotten a bunny rabbit for the classroom, you and your team members decide to make bunnies at small-group time. Since there are three of you, you decide on three different sets of materials to use. Describe the materials, what you say to the children to get them started, and what kinds of bunnies might result from each small group.

l) Even though Sasha is chronologically 3½ years old, developmentally he is about 1½ years old. After each key experience in representation, describe the expectations you would have for him, keeping in mind that, like any 1½-year-old, he can observe and understand far more than he can do or talk about.

1. Recognizing objects by sound, touch, taste, and smell

2. Imitating actions and sounds

3. Relating models, photographs, and pictures to real places and things

4. Role playing

5. Making models

6. Making drawings and paintings

7. Observing that spoken words can be written down and read back

13. Observing, experiencing, and representing in a preschool classroom

Turn to the experiencing and representing checklist in **Young Children in Action** on pages 308-9. Spend time in a preschool classroom looking for the items on the checklist and checking off the ones you find.

a) Describe this classroom's greatest strengths in providing children with opportunities for experiencing and representing.

b) If this were your classroom, describe the changes you would make to provide more opportunities for experiencing and representing.

14. Representation issues to ponder

a) Why do children represent?

b) Do adults represent? If so, why and how?

c) Preschoolers generally like their representations, but adults often say, "Mine isn't very good." Why?

d) How does a well-organized classroom affect children's opportunities to experience and represent?

e) Is it possible for people to represent things or situations they have not experienced? Why or why not? If so, how?

f) What is the relationship between language and representation?

g) Would children's ability to represent vary from culture to culture? Why or why not? If so, how?

h) What is the relationship between representation and reading? Between representation and mathematics?

i) What is the difference between "real" materials and "abstract" materials?

j) What is the relationship between imitation and role play?

k) Once children begin drawing and painting, will they continue to imitate? Why or why not?

15. Representation projects

a) Represent an experience you have had. Use two of the following media: mime, dance, sculpture, drawing, painting, photography, drama, music, or writing.

b) Start a collection of children's representations. Include the child's name and age, and the date on each item.

c) Go to an art museum and do the following:

    1. Find two paintings on the same subject by two different artists. How are their representations the same? Different?

    2. Stand in a room of abstract paintings. What do they represent?

    3. Look at Greek artifacts and Egyptian artifacts. How are the representations of these two cultures the same? How are they different?

    4. What is your favorite part of the museum? Why?

d) Make a list of all the representations you see throughout one day.

Ballpark Definitions

balls — *peas*	Leftyalls — *Southerners*	remills — *fulfills*
ballpark —*peanut*	lip — *oil*	Right — *Central*
bushfuls — *handfuls*	loamy — *crumbly*	ruff — *full*
chopper — *snack*	loop — *food*	shingle deckers — *roof tops*
clamor — *habit*	mamford — *protein*	shipped — *shelled*
clamp — *plant*	maypole — *spring*	shives — *slaves*
clips — *stems*	mini — *small*	silter — *raise*
cloister — *mature*	mits — *pegs*	sled — *fed*
Crafica — *Africa*	nippy — *fresh*	sreboog balls — *goober peas*
cram — *bury*	overbeak — *underground*	stew — *grow*
crop — *source*	overgrown — *adult*	stoves — *amounts*
farm — *seed*	ozo — *air*	tattoed — *pulled up*
flack — *field*	pantry — *country*	tempo — *daily*
flappers — *flowers*	park — *nut*	termitters — *vitamins*
flukes — *soldiers*	pestering — *harvesting*	Terras — *States*
Free World — *America*	phase — *size*	Tied Terras — *United States*
gumble — *legume*	phed — *dry*	till — *soil*
Headbands — *Indians*	piaget — *fall*	tilt — *wilt*
heels — *contains*	pippen — *ripen*	tipa creep — *lima beans*
hued — *colored*	pished — *threshed*	tracer — *machine*
jerney — *trip*	ploppy — *sandy*	trap — *produce*
Keeneys — *Yankees*	rakers — *gardeners*	unpurpled — *unsaturated*
leds — *eat*	raw — *war*	Yonder — *North*
Left — *South*		

Films and Publications

Films

Experiencing and Representing

[PS110] Set of four 16mm films; color, sound; 48 min total
These programs demonstrate the importance of direct experience and representational play and show how the preschool environment can promote both experience and representation. In each section, two teachers discuss specific activities from their classroom and demonstrate a variety of teaching strategies.

Part I—A Way Children Learn
[PS111] (12 min)
Shows a variety of classroom activities in which children spontaneously represent things they've done or seen. Teachers discuss how children at different stages of intellectual development vary in their ability to hold details in mind and depict them in space and time. They also discuss the importance of representational play for later cognitive and academic development.

Part II—Starting with Direct Experience
[PS112] (12 min)
Some materials teachers can provide and techniques they can use to promote concrete experience in the preschool classroom as a basis for later representational activity.

Part III—From Direct Experience to Representation
[PS113] (8 min)
Teaching strategies to help children represent their experiences: sequencing activities from the concrete to the abstract; structuring the classroom in a nondirective way to encourage children to represent ideas and experiences in a variety of media.

Part IV—Strategies for Supporting Representational Activity
[PS114] (16 min)
Teaching strategies that encourage children to add detail and complexity to their representations; shows the process of taking dictation from the child to stimulate verbal representation and to help the child learn that writing is a way of representing spoken language.

Observing Role Play

[PS144] 16mm film; black & white, sound; 15 min
Scenes from the High/Scope Preschool are used to illustrate a sequence of role-play situations teachers can recognize and encourage in children: pretending to be someone else, sharing a pretend situation with another person, using one object to stand for another, imitating actions or sounds, using language to describe a pretend situation, using language appropriate to a role, remaining in a role-play situation for a significant amount of time.

The Block Area

[PS191] Set of five color filmstrips and cassette tapes; 38.7 min total

4. A Place to Represent Things
(8.7 min)
Structures children build in the block area—roads, sidewalks, barns, garages, houses—and ways a teacher can respond to and support this important work of young children.

Guidelines for Evaluating Activities

[PS150] Set of three 16mm films; black & white, sound; 58 min total; discussion guides included
These programs demonstrate alternative ways teachers can plan and carry out activities with a group of preschool children. Each program shows two contrasting styles of structuring and leading a group activity, using similar materials but different teaching methods and goals. Useful for stimulating discussion of teaching styles and educational philosophies. An accompanying observation guide offers criteria by which to evaluate and revise classroom activities. Also included is a trainer's supplement that discusses the films in terms of the criteria in the guide and offers suggestions for revising the activities.

Contrasting Teaching Styles: Small-Group Time
[PS151] (18 min)

Contrasting Teaching Styles: Work Time, the Art Area
[PS152] (22 min)

Contrasting Teaching Styles: Circle Time
[PS153] (18 min)

Representation

16mm films with live action; color, sound
Children portray, or "represent," their thoughts in many ways—for example, they draw and paint, tell or write stories, make models, enact familiar scenes. Representation enriches experience and helps to clarify thought—it is a crucial factor in development, as these two films demonstrate.

Children Make Representations for Many Reasons
[EE202] (16 min)
An overview of representation—why it is important in an educational setting, what kinds of representation are likely to occur throughout the children's day. The film pinpoints the role of representational activity in stimulating and clarifying thinking and in developing a more detailed and accurate conception of reality.

Teachers Make Representing a Thinking Process
[EE203] (17 min)
This film depicts the role of the teacher in implementing representation as a formal curriculum component. It demonstrates that representation is a creative process satisfying for both teacher and child and stresses the role of the teacher as a facilitator and observer of children's representations. It also shows some ways teachers can use questions, participation in children's activities, and additional materials to help children expand their representational activities and thus their thinking.

Publications

Writing and Reading (#6)
Author: O. B. Hsu; booklet (40 pages); 1977

The guide contains a plan for developing writing and reading abilities in children based on the following premises: 1) that writing and reading are best learned together; 2) that the child's initiation into literacy is a matter of discovering the connection between spoken and written language; 3) that the child discovers this connection best when personal experiences are the basis for the first attempts at writing and reading. Classroom writing activities can include dictating, tracing, copying, and eventually writing independently about the child's personal experiences. Reading begins with the child's own writing and subsequently includes writings by friends and printed materials. Strategies for extending children's stories and encouraging reading comprehension are also given. The appendices have detailed progressions of writing and reading abilities in relation to Piaget's developmental stages as well as criteria for evaluating quality and content in children's stories.

Write or call the High/Scope Foundation, 600 North River Street, Ypsilanti, MI 48197, (313) 485-2000 to obtain information on ordering these materials.

8/Classification

Preschool children enjoy classifying—exploring and talking about the attributes of things, discovering similarities, putting things that are the same together, talking about things that are the same and things that are different. As preschoolers begin to classify, they begin to use logical thinking skills to distinguish characteristics of things and to sort and arrange them according to these characteristics. Since preschoolers are naturally eager to classify, it is up to adults to provide children with really interesting materials and to encourage children to talk about attributes, similarities, and differences.

1. Classification: Definitions, examples, rationale

Read pages 191-95 in **Young Children in Action**. Then do exercises *a-e*.

a) Define and illustrate the following terms:

1. Graphic collections

2. Nongraphic collections

3. Sorting

4. Class inclusion

5. Multiple class membership

6. Multiple attributes

b) Give at least one example each of a child exhibiting the following classificatory behaviors:

   1. Making different responses to different objects

   2. Exploring attributes

   3. Using class names

   4. Making graphic collections

   5. Sorting by identity

   6. Sorting by similarity

c) Briefly define classification and why it is important for preschoolers to have classification experiences.

d) Explain how each of the following social institutions uses classification:

   1. Museums

   2. Libraries

   3. Post offices

   4. School systems

e) How does the following exercise from *Brain Boosters* by David Webster (p 43)* call upon classification skills? Would this exercise be more appropriate for preschoolers or adults? Explain.

All of these are Fubbyloofers—

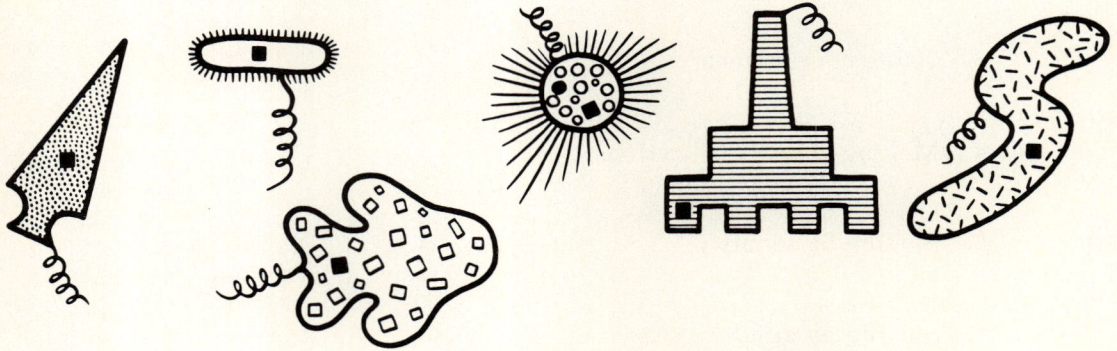

None of these is a Fubbyloofer—

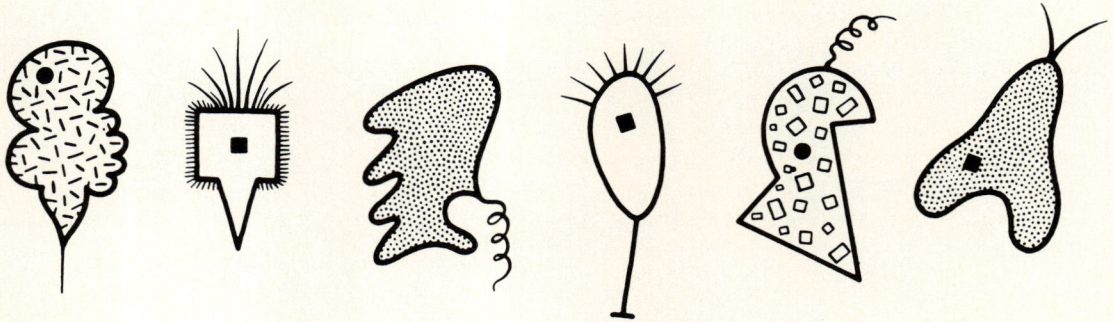

Which of these are Fubbyloofers?

---

* Copyright © 1966 by David Webster. Reprinted by permission of David Webster and Natural History Press, Garden City, N.Y.

2. Child study: Children's developing classification skills

The idea of this exercise is to see for yourself how different children classify, each according to his or her level of cognitive development. Of course, you will not be teaching children to classify. They will be teaching you about how they classify. They will be showing you what they understand about the attributes of objects and how objects go together. In this exercise, you will be presenting some children with a number of red and yellow pencils, some long, some short, some sharpened, some unsharpened. You will ask each child to make piles of pencils that go together. Whichever sorting scheme he or she chooses, each child must remember the criterion for sorting without being misled by other differences and similarities.

Between the ages of two to about four, children display only rudimentary understanding of classification concepts. Two typical forms of classification behavior by young children during this period are the making of "graphic collections" and "chaining." Making a graphic collection involves separating objects at random with no apparent criterion in mind, other than, "These things go together because they are together." "Chaining" consists of putting objects in a string or in a line instead of in groups. A typical explanation would be, "This cow goes with the house because they are both wood. This rubber horse goes with the cow because they are both animals. This eraser goes with the horse because they are both rubber." Each decision determines the rationale for the next, rather than each decision depending upon some preconceived scheme or plan for sorting.

When children do begin to use logic in their classification activities, their first attempts usually consist of many small groups or piles rather than a few large ones. When presented the pencils spoken of earlier and given the instructions, "Put things together that go together," young children are apt to make eight separate piles of identical pencils—the long, red, sharpened pencils; the long, yellow, sharpened pencils; the long, red, unsharpened pencils; the long, yellow, unsharpened pencils; the short, yellow, sharpened pencils; the short, red, sharpened pencils; the short, red, unsharpened pencils; and the short, yellow, unsharpened pencils. Children who sort this way have progressed in logical development to understanding that things go together if they have common attributes. They also have the "mental flexibility" to devise a plan and complete it.

At a slightly more advanced level, a child usually makes a smaller number of groups—the long, sharpened pencils (red and yellow); the long, unsharpened pencils (red and yellow); the short, sharpened pencils (red and yellow); and the short, unsharpened pencils (red and yellow).

At a still higher level, a child sorts objects into even fewer groups—the sharpened pencils (long-short, red-yellow) and the unsharpened pencils (long-short, red-yellow). Such children have developed several classification skills. They know that objects and events can be classified according to their attributes; they can recognize a commonality among otherwise dissimilar objects; and once they have chosen a criterion for placing objects in a group, they are not distracted.

Find five children between the ages of three and five years with whom you can work individually for at least 15 minutes. Include your "child-study" child.

Gather together a set of the following materials: two long red pencils, unsharpened; two long red pencils, sharpened; two short red pencils, unsharpened; two short red pencils, sharpened; two long yellow pencils, unsharpened; two long yellow pencils, sharpened; two short yellow pencils, unsharpened; two short yellow pencils, sharpened.

a) Ask each child the following questions in the order given and record each child's answers and your observations in the chart below:

- What are all the things you can tell me about these pencils? Tell me as many things about them as you can.

- Can you put all the pencils together that go together? Show me how you would put the pencils together that go together. (Look for graphic collections, chains, groups of identical pencils, groups of similar pencils.)

- Good. Now let's put all the pencils back into one big pile. Can you put them together again in a different way? Show me how you can make some different piles of pencils that go together.

Child	Attributes of Pencils Child Named	Groups of Pencils Child Made First Time	Groups of Pencils Child Made Second Time
Name: Age:			
Name: Age:			
Name: Age:			
Name: Age:			
Name: Age:			

180

b) Which child has the most advanced understanding of classification? How can you tell?

c) Which child has the least advanced understanding of classification? How can you tell?

d) Do you remember any sorting and matching you did as a child?

e) Review and discuss exercises *a-d* with your team members.

3. Recognizing key experiences in classification

Classification occurs wherever children and objects come together. The trick for adults is to learn to recognize the classification process as it occurs. Listed below are the key experiences in classification for preschool-aged children. As you read through each of the following classroom situations, you will decide which key experience(s) in classification it illustrates.

Key Experiences: Classification

- Investigating and describing the attributes of things

- Noticing and describing how things are the same and how they are different; sorting and matching

- Using and describing objects in different ways

- Talking about the characteristics something does *not* possess or the class it does *not* belong to

- Holding more than one attribute in mind at a time

- Distinguishing between "some and all"

---

a) At Mr. Barnum's small-group time the children are using a variety of materials to make models and pictures of animals and performers they saw at the circus.
   "Look at my tail," says Robert to Henry.
   "I did mine different. My tiger has one tail right here on his back," says Henry, showing his to Robert with satisfaction.
   Identify the key experience(s) in classification.

b) "Look at my puzzle, Teacher. See this piece can stand up like this." Marketta stands a cat puzzle piece on the rug. "And it can lie down flat like this in the puzzle, too." She fits the cat piece back into the puzzle. "It can stand up and look around, and it can go to bed."

Identify the key experience(s) in classification.

c) At planning time Jack made a plan to "play with those long round things. You know, the ones with the rounds you can put together and take apart again."

"You mean the Tinkertoys?" asks his teacher.

"Yeh! I'm gonna play with the Tinkertoys," replies Jack.

"Identify the key experience(s) in classification.

d) "Put that truck back, Rocky," Joey advises. "It doesn't have any wheels."

Identify the key experience(s) in classification.

e) "Look at my building, Teacher," Lynnette calls excitedly. "See, these people's all the same, so they go in here; and these people's all the same, so they go in here. And these blocks all fit together, so they go here; and these chimneys are just like these chimneys, so they go here."

Identify the key experience(s) in classification.

f) Outside Kimi and Angela find a caterpillar.

"He's fuzzy."

"He's got some long spiky things sticking out his eyes."

"He's tickling my hand."

"Where's his feet? Oh, here they are underneath. They're all black except for these red ones."

"Let's put him in the sandbox."

Identify the key experience(s) in classification.

g) Jeff very proudly brings a box to snack time. "It's my birthday, and I helped my mom make these cookies. There's some for us and there's some for the other table. There's cookies for all the kids and I made 'em too. My mom said each person can take two!"

Identify the key experience(s) in classification.

h) It's Mia's first day in school and Lois is helping Mia clean up in the art area. "Okay, now look," says Lois. "You put these sharp scissors here with these other sharp scissors and I'll get all the round-end scissors and put 'em here in this can, okay Mia?"

 Identify the key experience(s) in classification.

i) "Here's what I'm going to do," announces Willa at planning time. "I'm going to dress up in that special party dress with the lace and the big, big skirt, and I'm going to church for a wedding."

 Identify the key experience(s) in classification.

j) As Lauren passes out the napkins at snack time, she announces, "It's too hot for a sweater today, so I'm giving napkins to just people with no sweaters on. Too bad if you're wearing a sweater."

 Identify the key experience(s) in classification.

k) As Anita cleans up in the house area she sings to herself, "I'm putting in the red chips, the red chips, the red chips. I'm putting in the red chips, red chips, red chips. I'm putting in the red . . . "

 Identify the key experience(s) in classification.

l) Matt is dressing his teddy bear in doll's clothes when Anil joins him with another teddy bear. Matt warns him, "Some of these clothes are too small. They don't fit cause our bears are too big. But some of them are okay. Here, try this one."

 Identify the key experience(s) in classification.

m) At outside time a group of children are using an old board for a ramp to race cars down. After a while they get tired of this activity so they decide to use the board for a seesaw. Not everyone who wants to seesaw can fit on, so they change it into a bridge to crawl under and over.

 Identify the key experience(s) in classification.

n) At circle time Jessie and Skye announce, "We're sitting together cause we both have on the same knee socks. See they're green and they have flowers up the sides."
Identify the key experience(s) in classification.

o) Visit a preschool classroom. Look for examples of each of the key experiences in classification and clearly describe each one.

Key Experience	Classroom Examples
Investigating and describing the attributes of things	
Noticing and describing how things are the same and how they are different; sorting and matching	
Using and describing objects in different ways	
Talking about the characteristics something does *not* possess or the class it does *not* belong to	
Holding more than one attribute in mind at a time	
Distinguishing between "some" and "all"	

p) Review and discuss exercises *a-o* with your team members.

4. Providing opportunities for classification through room arrangement

Preschool classrooms can be arranged and equipped to encourage children to classify. Storing crayons by color gives children the opportunity to sort and match at clean-up time, for example. For this exercise, look at each of the classroom photographs in **Young Children in Action** listed below and write down which key experience(s) in classification the room arrangement or equipment is providing. See if your team members agree with you.

Classroom Photograph	Classification Key Experience(s) Provided
Page 37 (bottom): Block shelf looking into house area	
Page 41: House area equipment	
Page 43 (left): Art area materials	
Page 93: Small-group-time materials	
Page 95 (both): Outdoor equipment	
Page 97: Musical instruments	
Page 128: Blocks	

Classroom Photograph	Classification Key Experience(s) Provided
Page 132: House area materials	
Page 191: Quiet area materials	
Page 200: Block area materials	
Page 225: Quiet area materials	
Page 243: Small-group-time materials	
Page 257: Real baby	
Page 279 (bottom): House area equipment	

5. Classification: Adding content to conversations

Knowing the classification key experiences helps adults see what children are doing and, as a result, adds content to their conversations with children. For example, instead of saying to a child who is sharing the pinecones, "Aren't these pinecones nice?" an adult aware of the classification key experience *investigating and describing the attributes of things* might say, "Aren't these pinecones brown and prickly?"

a) Expand each of the following conversational statements by adding content to emphasize the classification key experience indicated. Each statement refers to a photograph in **Young Children in Action** that helps clarify the conversation.

1. Page 192: "Denise, isn't that a lovely pile you've made." (Investigating and describing the attributes of things)

2. Page 34: "Why, Mike, those two towers were magnificent!" (Noticing and describing how things are the same and how they are different)

3. Page 195: "What a good idea, Sam. When you put the beans in there they do that and when you put them in here they don't." (Using and describing objects in different ways)

4. Page 77: "That's not going to work, Jamison." (Talking about the characteristics something does *not* possess)

5. Page 191: "Yep, they both have 'em, Timmy." (Noticing and describing how things are the same and how they are different)

6. Page 179 (left): "Isn't she a cute baby, children!" (Investigating and describing the attributes of things)

7. Page 170 (middle): "See, yours is just like this." (Noticing and describing how things are the same and how they are different)

8. Page 214: "Let's take them out of the box but just wash the dirty ones." (Distinguishing between "some" and "all")

9. Page 90: "Can you find another one that's just like this one?" (Holding more than one attribute in mind at a time)

b) Make up your own conversational statements emphasizing classification to accompany the following photographs:

1. Page 211: (Investigating and describing the attributes of things)

2. Page 200: (Noticing and describing how things are the same and how they are different)

3. Page 204: (Using and describing objects in different ways)

c) Review and discuss exercises a-b with your team members.

6. Using small-group time to find out how children classify

One way to find out how children classify is to plan small-group times around the classification key experiences. As children work with materials on the task set forth, adults can watch to see what each child does. Review small-group time procedures and suggestions on pages 92-94, 198-99, 204-6, 208-9 in **Young Children in Action.**

a) In this exercise, together with your team members, you are planning a small-group time based on the classification key experience *investigating and describing the attributes of things.* The children in your small group are Elise (4½), Marketta (3), Mike (3), Troy (3), and Juanita (4).

1. List the materials you will need for each child.

2. How will you get this small-group time started? What will you say to let the children know what to do with the materials? How will you communicate with Juanita who speaks only Spanish?

3. Describe three different things you might see children doing with the materials.

4. Describe three things you might do to support and encourage children in this activity.

5. How would you draw this activity to a meaningful end?

b) Together with your team members, you are planning a small-group time based on the classification key experience *noticing and describing how things are the same and how they are different, sorting and matching.* The children in your small group are Brenda (4½), Corey (3½), Michelle (4½), Sam (3), and Sasha (3½).

1. List the materials you will need for each child.

2. How will you get this small-group time started? What will you say to let the children know what to do with the materials?

3. Describe three different things you might see children doing with materials (include what Sasha might do).

4. Describe three things you might do to support and encourage children in this activity.

5. How would you draw this small-group time to a meaningful end?

c) In this exercise, together with your team members, you are planning a small-group time based on the classification key experience *using and describing objects in different ways*. The children in your small group are Clarice (3), Denise (3), Jamison (4), Raymond (4), Timmy (4½).

   1. List the materials you will need for each child.

2. How will you get this small-group time started? What will you say to let the children know what to do with the materials?

3. Describe three different things you might see children doing with materials.

4. Describe three things you might do to support and encourage children in this activity.

5. How would you draw this small-group time to a meaningful end?

7. Classification at work time

Once adults are alert to classification key experiences, they can see them occurring throughout work time and in most other situations where children work with materials. The question then becomes, How do adults act on these observations? Review *Suggestions for Adults* in **Young Children in Action** on pages 195-215. Then read through the following work-time situations and do the exercises with your team members.

a) "Look at my puzzle, Teacher. See, this piece can stand up like this." Marketta stands a cat puzzle piece on the rug. "And it can lie down flat like this in the puzzle too." She fits the cat piece back into the puzzle. "It can stand up and it can go to bed."

  1. Identify the classification key experience(s).

  2. Suggest strategies to support, encourage, or extend the experience(s).

b) "Look at my building, Teacher," Lynnette calls excitedly. "See, these people's all the same, and they can go in here; and these people's all the same, so they can go in here. And these blocks all fit together, so they go here; and these chimneys are just like these chimneys, so they go here."

  1. Identify the classification key experience(s).

  2. Suggest strategies to support, encourage, or extend the experience(s).

c) You see that Timmy is discouraged about something in the art area so you ask him what's wrong. "Well, I want to make a motorcycle that looks just like this one," says Timmy, showing you a magazine picture of a motorcycle. "But mine doesn't look the same, see," he says, showing you the picture he's drawing with magic markers. "Mine looks different. I want mine to have all those things."

1. Identify the classification key experience(s).

2. Suggest strategies to support, encourage, or extend the experience(s).

d) Troy is at the easel but so far hasn't gotten much paint on the paper. Instead he is feeling the paint brush bristles against his hand, cheek, and lips. He's dipping his fingers into the paint jar, stirring with the brushes, and using the brushes to paint his hands. When he does try putting paint on the paper, he stops to watch the drips drip all the way down from the top of the paper to the bottom.

1. Identify the classification key experience(s).

2. Suggest strategies to support, encourage, or extend the experience(s).

e) Brenda is busily digging through the dress-up shoes saying, "yep" or "nope" as she comes to each one.

    1.   Identify the classification key experience(s).

    2.   Suggest strategies to support, encourage, or extend the experience(s).

f) At the workbench, Corey is making a "wind surfer." He uses the hammer to pound in nails, to pull out a crooked nail, and to measure the length of the second board he needs.

    1.   Identify the classification key experience(s).

    2.   Suggest strategies to support, encourage, or extend the experience(s).

g) "Look, Teacher," calls Sam, "we're playing all the instruments. Listen to this." Sam, Mike, Denise, Corey, and Clarice play you a "concert" on the tambourines, triangles, drums, and bells.

    1.   Identify the classification key experience(s).

2. Suggest strategies to support, encourage, or extend the experience(s).

8. Restructuring songs, games, and field trips to stress classification

Many children's songs, games, and outings can be altered somewhat to emphasize classification.

a) In **Young Children in Action,** review suggestions on pages 197-98, 204, 211, and 213.

b) With your team members, select a *song* to sing with children at circle time that can be altered to emphasize a classification key experience.

1. Write the lyrics of the song as it is traditionally sung.

2. List the classification key experience you will emphasize.

3. Revise the lyrics of the song, emphasizing the classification key experience you selected.

c) With your team members, select a *game* to play with children at outside time that can be altered to emphasize a classification key experience.

   1. Describe the game as it is traditionally played.

2. List the classification key experience you will emphasize.

3. Describe the alterations you would make in the game to emphasize the classification key experience you selected.

d) You and your team members are planning a *field trip* that will emphasize classification. So far you have talked about going to the dairy farm, to the grocery store, for a walk around the block, to the natural history museum, or to the pet shop.

1. Select one of the above places to visit that you think would provide many opportunities for classification.

2. List the classification key experiences you will emphasize and describe what the children will do to experience them.

Classification Key Experience	What the Children Will Do

Classification Key Experience	What the Children Will Do

9. Observing classification in a preschool classroom

Using the classification checklist in **Young Children in Action,** pages 309-10, observe a preschool classroom and check off all the items that apply.

a) What are the major strengths of this classroom in the area of classification?

b) If this were your classroom, what changes would you make to provide more classification key experiences for children?

10. Classification issues to ponder

a) Can adults teach classification skills to preschoolers? For example, can adults teach classification by showing preschoolers how to sort crayons into two groups—sharp crayons and dull crayons? Why or why not?

b) What is the difference between teaching children how to sort into two groups and providing children with experiences in noticing and describing how things are the same and how they are different?

c) How are the key experiences in classification related to active learning? To language? To experiencing and representing?

d) If a group of preschoolers grew up on a lush tropical island without adult intervention, would they develop classification skills? If so, how? If not, why not?

e) What is the role of adults in the development of preschoolers' ability to classify?

11. Classification projects

a) Start a classification album. As you work with children and materials, photograph or sketch examples of children sorting and matching. Label each photo or sketch with the child's name and age, the date, and the location.

b) Design an active-learning exercise that would help adults understand what classification is. Try it out on some adults.

c) Construct a toy or design a game that would provide classification key experiences for preschoolers. Have your "child-study" child try out the toy or game.

Films

Guidelines for Evaluating Activities

[PS150] Set of three 16mm films; black & white, sound; 58 min total; discussion guides included

These programs demonstrate alternative ways teachers can plan and carry out activities with a group of preschool children. Each program shows two contrasting styles of structuring and leading a group activity, using similar materials but different teaching methods and goals. Useful for stimulating discussion of teaching styles and educational philosophies. An accompanying observation guide offers criteria by which to evaluate and revise classroom activities. Also included is a trainer's supplement that discusses the films in terms of the criteria in the guide and offers suggestions for revising the activities.

Contrasting Teaching Styles: Small-Group Time
[PS151] (18 min)

Contrasting Teaching Styles: Work Time, the Art Area
[PS152] (22 min)

Contrasting Teaching Styles: Circle Time
[PS153] (18 min)

Cognitive Development Series

16mm films, color, sound

Each film in this series deals with a different kind of thinking process—classifying, seriating, temporal thinking, spatial understanding—and shows a sequence of curriculum goals and corresponding key experiences for elementary-aged students. Each goal and experience is described briefly and illustrated with classroom examples.

1. Classification—A Sequence of Exercises
[EE211] (25 min)

Children gradually develop the ability to group things on the basis of similarities and differences in attributes and use; they learn to make and identify connections.

Write or call the High/Scope Foundation, 600 North River Street, Ypsilanti, MI 48197, (313) 485-2000 to obtain information on ordering these materials.

9/Seriation

Seriation, finding order in difference, is the process of arranging objects or ideas in order (either physically or mentally) according to variations in one of their properties. Seriation develops as children grow physically, logically, and experientially. Preschool children are not yet able to master the logic of seriation, but they are very involved in comparing, arranging a few things in order, and fitting ordered sets of objects together. While these skills do not constitute seriation, they are important first steps.

1. Defining seriation

Review pages 217-19 in **Young Children in Action,** then answer the following questions:

a) What is seriation?

b) Why is it important for preschoolers to have opportunities to make comparisons, arrange things in order, and fit ordered sets of objects together?

c) While preschoolers are not yet able to seriate, adults seriate both tangible objects and abstract ideas according to a wide variety of dimensions. For examples of adult seriation, arrange the following sets of objects according to the dimensions given.

1. Rank the following military commissions from the lowest to the highest rank:

second lieutenant	Lowest 1.
lieutenant general	2.
captain	3.
general	4.
colonel	5.
major	6.
major general	7.
lieutenant colonel	8.
first lieutenant	9.
brigadier general	Highest 10.

2. You've won free round-trip airline tickets from the airport nearest you to any one of seven cities:

Denver, Colorado   Cincinnati, Ohio
Boston, Massachusetts   Seattle, Washington
Washington, D.C.   New York, New York
Miami, Florida

In considering which city to visit, *first* rank the cities according to their distances from your airport.

Farthest from your airport 1.
2.
3.
4.
5.
6.
Nearest to your airport 7.

Second, rank the same seven cities according to desirability.

Most like to visit 1.
2.
3.
4.
5.
6.
Least like to visit 7.

Third, rank the cities according to the average nightly cost of hotel rooms in each city.

Miami $64   Least expensive 1.
Cincinnati $25   2.
Washington, D.C. $69   3.
Seattle $50   4.
Boston $85   5.
New York $91   6.
Denver $68   Most expensive 7.

Finally, after considering these three factors—distance, desirability, hotel costs—you decide to visit _____ . Enjoy your trip!

d) Describe a situation in your life in which you have used seriation.

205

2. Recognizing seriation key experiences

Review the seriation key experiences listed below and described in **Young Children in Action** pages 219-26.

Key Experiences: Seriation

- Making comparisons
- Arranging several things in order and describing their relations

- Fitting one ordered set of objects to another through trial and error

---

In exercises *a-i*, you will consider some classroom situations in your preschool and decide which seriation key experience is occurring in each situation.

a) It's clean-up time. Lynnette is putting away a big pile of spoons singing as she goes— "Here's a soup spoon. Here's an eating spoon. Here's a baby spoon. Here's a soup spoon. Here's an eating spoon. Here's a baby spoon."
   Identify the seriation key experience.

b) "Teacher, help me. That piece was easy to saw but this piece is much harder. You do some, okay?"
   Identify the seriation key experience.

c) Timmy and Elise are setting up a post office in the block area.
   "Now before all the people come," Timmy instructs Elise, "we have to have all these papers ready. Now, we're gonna put these big papers here in these big envelopes, like this." Timmy puts a big paper into a big manila envelope. "Then we gotta put these not-so-big papers in these envelopes," indicating the medium-sized envelopes. "And we got to put these little bitty papers in these little bitty envelopes."
   "Yeh," says Elise, "these are the birthday party invitations."
   Identify the seriation key experience.

d) "Happy birthday, dear Sasha. Happy birthday to you," everyone sings as Sasha blows out the four candles on his cupcake.
   "I wish I had Sasha's cupcake," says Jamison, "cause his has more candles on it."
   Identify the seriation key experience.

e) Brenda is hunting through the extra mitten box for some mittens to wear in the snow for outside time. "Look, Teacher, here are some big ones for you." Brenda proves her point by putting them on your hands. "And here are some tiny ones for my baby." She puts these on her dolly. "And here are some nice red ones just for me." She slips them on and races out into the snow.

    Identify the seriation key experience.

f) Elise has built a big block fence for the farm animals. "Here's where all the daddies go," she says putting all the daddy animals together in one corner. "Here's a place for all the mommies, and here's where all the babies go except when they're hungry. Then they find their moms."

    Identify the seriation key experience.

g) "I like this truck better than yours because it's bigger and it has bigger wheels," boasts Jamison.

    "Well, I like mine better because it's tinier and it can go into lots of places like this one right here," replies Timmy.

    Identify the seriation key experience.

h) "Look at this picture I made, Teacher. This one's my dad. He's the biggest. This one's my mom. She's in the middle. And this teeny, tiny one's my baby brother. He's just a dot!"

    Identify the seriation key experience.

i) Sam and Mike are looking at a Halloween picture book together.

    "That ghost sure looks scary," says Mike.

    "Yeh, but this witch looks scarier to me. Look at her mean face. She's scarier all right."

    Identify the seriation key experience.

j) Turn to the following pages in **Young Children in Action**. Briefly describe what you see and what seriation key experience is represented.

Page	Brief Description	Seriation Key Experience
41		
43 (left)		
217		
219		
220 (bottom)		
220 (top)		
222		
224		
225		

k) Review and discuss exercises *a-j* with your team members.

3. Providing materials to compare, arrange, and fit together

To provide seriation key experiences for preschoolers, it is necessary to have a variety of materials that children can compare, arrange, and fit together. Do exercises *a* and *b* with your team members.

a) Turn to the list of comparative terms on page 220 in **Young Children in Action.** You decide to make these types of materials available in your preschool classroom. Write down your ideas in the following chart. Include both found and commercial materials.

Materials to Compare	Art Area	Quiet Area	House Area	Block Area	Music Area	Outside Area
Heavier/Lighter						
Sharper/Blunter						
Rougher/Smoother						
Wetter/Drier						
Louder/Softer						
Harder/Softer						
Bigger/Smaller						
Thicker/Thinner						

b) Choose three of the materials you have selected and describe and/or illustrate how you would label them to emphasize a seriation key experience.

4. Child study: Seriation

In **Young Children in Action,** review the list of materials in three or four sizes on pages 222-23 and the list of sets of materials that fit together on page 226. From each list, select some sets of materials that you can actually find and use, and collect these materials. You will also need three children with whom you can spend at least ten minutes apiece. They should be of the ages shown in the chart below. One should be your "child-study" child.

a) Present each child with each set of materials and record what each child does and says in the chart below.

Child and Materials

What Child Did with Materials

(three-year-old)

Name:

Age:

Materials of graduated sizes:

Materials that fit together:

(four-year-old)

Name:

Age:

Materials of graduated sizes:

Materials that fit together:

(five-year-old)

Name:

Age:

Materials of graduated sizes:

Materials that fit together:

b) From your observations, what conclusions can you draw about the development of seriation skills?

c) Review and discuss exercises *a* and *b* with your team members.

5. Including seriation in everyday conversations and questions

Seriation, like classification, can lend content to adults' conversations with children. For example, instead of saying to a child sharing some pinecones, "Aren't these pinecones nice?" an adult aware of the seriation key experience *making comparisons* might say, "Aren't these pinecones nice? This big one is light brown and this little one is dark brown."

a) Expand each of the following conversations by adding content to emphasize the seriation key experience indicated. Each statement refers to a photograph in **Young Children in Action.**

1. Page 41 "Denise, you're doing a nice job cleaning up." (Fitting one set of objects to another through trial and error)

2. Page 43 (Left) "You sure can stretch your elastic, Clarice." (Making comparisons)

3. Page 47 "My goodness! Two people sawing on one piece of wood." (Making comparisons)

4. Page 51 "These logs look like steps." (Arranging several things in order and describing their relations)

5. Page 54 "I think the guinea pig is hungry. It's good you each have a carrot for him." (Making comparisons)

6. Page 219 "Which teddy bear are you going to play with, Brenda?" (Arranging several things in order and describing their relations)

b) To accompany the following photographs in **Young Children in Action,** make up your own conversation emphasizing seriation.

1. Page 220 (bottom) (Making comparisons)

2. Page 224 (Arranging several things in order and describing their relations)

3. Page 225 (Fitting one ordered set of objects to another through trial and error)

c) Review and discuss exercises *a* and *b* with your team members.

6. Observing seriation in a classroom

Using the seriation checklist on pages 310-11 in **Young Children in Action,** observe a preschool classroom, checking off the checklist items you see.

a) What are this classroom's strengths regarding seriation?

b) If this were your classroom, what changes would you make to provide more seriation key experiences for children?

7. Seriation issues to ponder

a) During what parts of the daily routine would you expect to see children seriating? Why?

b) What is the relationship between seriation and representing? Between seriation and language?

c) How does seriation affect your everyday life?

d) How is the nuclear arms race related to seriation?

e) What is "ordered difference"? Give some examples.

8. Seriation projects

a) Design and build a toy that provides seriation key experiences for preschoolers. Have your "child-study" child try it out.

b) Write and illustrate a children's story that includes seriation. Read it to your "child-study" child. See if he or she would like to dictate a similar story to you.

c) As you go through a day, make a list of all the examples of seriation you encounter and all the situations in which you use seriation.

Films and Publications

Films

Cognitive Development Series
16mm films, color, sound
Each film in this series deals with a different kind of thinking process—classifying, seriating, temporal thinking, spatial understanding—and shows a sequence of curriculum goals and corresponding key experiences for elementary-aged students. Each goal and experience is described briefly and illustrated with classroom examples.

2. Seriation—A Sequence of Exercises
[EE212] (25 min)
Children learn to order objects along a dimension—for example, saying which of two objects is bigger, or lining people up according to height.

Publications

Finding Order in Difference: Seriation in Elementary Curricula
Author: Charles Hohmann; reprint (3 pages); 1975.
This article defines seriation, gives examples of seriation in adult life, and traces the development of seriation skills in children.

Write or call the High/Scope Foundation, 600 North River Street, Ypsilanti, MI 48197, (313) 485-2000 to obtain information on ordering these materials.

10/Number

Preschoolers are equipped with pre-number logic and judgment. They are learning to make judgments about comparative amounts of things, to arrange things in one-to-one correspondence, and to count objects they are using. Their comparisons and counting will not always be correct by adult standards, but that's perfectly all right. The process of thinking about numbers in the best way they are able is what is important for preschoolers.

1. Understanding a preschooler's concept of number

To answer the following questions, review pages 228-30 in **Young Children in Action.**

a) What is one-to-one correspondence?

b) List at least three sets of items you use every day that correspond one-to-one. (For example, one cup for each saucer.)

c) What is conservation of number?

d) Referring to the graphic on page 229 in **Young Children in Action,** if you asked a preschool child which row had more things in it, row A or B, what would you expect the child to say? Why?

e) Referring to the same graphic, if you asked a preschool child which row had more things in it, row A or row E, what would you expect the child to say? Why?

f) Read the brief description of Piaget's experiments with vases and flowers and with bottles and glasses on pages 229-30 in **Young Children in Action.** Why could the preschool child count six glasses and six bottles and still say there were more bottles than glasses?

g) If a child in your preschool classroom counted six bottles and six glasses but said there were more bottles than glasses, would you try to correct the child? Why or why not?

h) What do you recall about your own early experiences with numbers?

2. Recognizing number key experiences

Review the number key experiences listed below. Then turn to the pages in **Young Children in Action** that are listed in the following chart. Briefly describe what you see in each photograph and identify the number key experience(s) represented.

Key Experiences: Number

- Comparing amounts
- Counting objects
- Arranging two sets of objects in one-to-one correspondence

Page	Brief Description	Number Key Experience(s)
63 (both)		
177		
228		
230		
231		
233		
234 (both)		
235		
236		

3. Comparing amounts

Review pages 230-32 in **Young Children in Action.** Then answer the following questions about the number key experience *comparing amounts.*

a) What are continuous materials?

b) List as many continuous materials as you can think of that you would provide in the following work areas:

Area	Continuous Materials
House	
Block	
Art	
Quiet	
Outdoor	

c) What are discontinuous materials?

d) List at least three discontinuous materials you would put in each of the following work areas:

Area	Discontinuous Materials
House	
Block	
Art	
Quiet	
Construction	
Outdoor	

e) It's Timmy's birthday and his mother has sent in cupcakes decorated with chocolate chips. Each cupcake has eight chocolate chips, but they're arranged randomly so that each cupcake looks different. Lynnette is crying because she claims that Timmy's cupcake has more chocolate chips than hers.

    1. Why might Lynnette believe that Timmy's cupcake has more chocolate chips than hers, even though they both have eight chips?

2. Realizing that Lynnette's reasoning about amounts makes sense to her, how would you deal with the situation?

3. If the strategy you just outlined didn't work, what's a second strategy you might try?

f) Turn to the photograph on page 191 in **Young Children in Action.** Suppose the teacher, Mr. Dodd, is asking Jeff questions about the comparative amounts of things he sees. List at least six questions he could ask.

    1.

    2.

    3.

    4.

    5.

    6.

g) What if Mr. Dodd asked Jeff to decide which one has more legs, the zebra or the zebra plant, and Jeff answered, "The zebra plant." What might Mr. Dodd do or say next?

h) Sam is playing in the sandbox pouring sand from a one-pint butter tub into a one-quart syrup container. "Look, Teacher," he announces, "now I've got more," indicating that when the sand is in the syrup jar there is "more sand" than when the same amount of sand is in the butter tub.

   1. What might Sam's reasoning be?

   2. How would you respond?

i) Juanita is looking at a magazine picture showing two rooms in a house. You ask her which room has more furniture in it. "I don't know," she answers. Why might Juanita have answered this way?

j) Review and discuss exercises *a-i* with your team members.

4. Arranging two sets of objects in one-to-one correspondence

Review pages 232-35 in **Young Children in Action.** Then answer the following questions about the number key experience *arranging two sets of objects in one-to-one correspondence.* Do this exercise with your team members.

a) You are stocking your classroom with sets of objects that fit together in one-to-one correspondence. List at least three such sets for each of the work areas listed in the chart below.

Area	Materials
House	
Block	
Quiet	
Art	
Music	
Construction	
Outdoor	

b) Mike is making lots of little round balls out of playdough and sticking a toothpick into each one. What might you say to him?

c) At small-group time your group is making popcorn to share with two groups. How could you turn popcorn making and delivering into an experience in one-to-one correspondence?

d) At outside time the children have made a game to "Jack Be Nimble." At the words, "Jack jump over the candlestick," each child in turn jumps over a small stone. You and your teaching team decide to adapt this idea to a circle-time game involving one-to-one correspondence. How would you do it?

e) Elise insists that Marketta can't play dress-up with her and Denise because "there aren't enough dresses." How can you help the three girls solve this dilemma, using one-to-one correspondence?

5. Counting objects

Review pages 235-36 in **Young Children in Action.** Then answer the following questions about the number key experience *counting objects:*

a) What is the difference between rote counting and counting objects?

b) List four things adults need to understand about the counting abilities of preschoolers.

    1.

    2.

    3.

    4.

c) Every preschool classroom should be amply stocked with countable objects. Look at photographs on the following pages in **Young Children in Action.** List all the countable objects you see in each photograph.

Page	Countable Objects
34 (both pictures)	
37 (both)	
41	
52	
151	
225	

d) Turn back to Figure 1 on pages 54-59 in this study guide and reread the classroom observations. Suppose that you could relive the day described, and as you relived it, you decided to seize every opportunity that arose to encourage children to count objects. Briefly describe each potential counting situation.

Time Block	Counting Situations
Planning Time	
Work Time	
Clean-up Time	
Recall Time	
Small-Group Time	
Circle Time	
Outside Time	

e) Raymond comes up to you all excited. "Look how many fish I made in this picture, Teacher. One, two, three, five, six, ten. Ten fish!" How would you respond?

f) You're visiting a local preschool. The teacher is working with a small group of children at a table. "Who knows how many days there are in the week?" she asks.

"Two," answers a little girl, "today and the next day after today."

"No," says the teacher, "there are seven. Let's count them. Monday, Tuesday, . . ." She goes through the days of the week and the children repeat them after her.

1. How would you evaluate this learning situation as a counting experience?

2. What changes would you make in this activity before you used it in your own classroom?

g) Timmy and Raymond are hauling loads of sticks from the bushes to the sand pile. After showing you the first couple of loads and counting the sticks with you, they decide they want you to keep track of the number of sticks in each load. "After we count, you write down the numbers, okay?" Raymond asks. Realizing that neither Timmy nor Raymond can read numbers, how would you comply with this request?

h) Review and discuss exercises *a-g* with your team members.

6. Observing number experiences in a preschool classroom

Spend some time in a preschool classroom. Use the number checklist on page 311 in **Young Children in Action.** Check off the items that apply.

a) What are this classroom's strengths in providing number experiences?

b) If this were your classroom, what changes would you make in providing number experiences?

7. Child study: Number

Child's Name: _____   **Date:** _____

Child's Age: _____   **Location:** _____

- Considering what you already know about _____ from previous child studies, provide _____ with some countable materials you know _____ will enjoy. Watch to see what _____ does with these materials and record your observations.

- Based on your observations, how will you join _____ without disrupting the child's play and provide some number key experiences?

- What happened when you joined _____ ?

- What did you learn about _____'s concept of number?

8. Number issues to ponder

a) Why are many adults, teachers, and parents so concerned about teaching children to count?

b) In this age of calculators and computers, is it still necessary for preschoolers to have the number key experiences outlined in **Young Children in Action**? Why or why not?

c) Some preschool children learn to play the violin, cello, or piano, starting as early as age two. They are able to play complex rhythms even though they have no numerical understanding of quarternotes, halfnotes, and whole notes. Considering their number abilities and the fact that they are not yet able to read music, how are they able to do this?

9. Number projects

a) Borrow an electronic math game like Speak & Math or Dataman. Evaluate the game in terms of its appropriateness for preschoolers.

b) Design a math video game appropriate for preschoolers.

c) Visit a preschooler's music lesson. How is it a number experience for the child?

d) Find all the nursery rhymes you can that involve numbers. Recite or read them to your "child-study" child. Together, make up your own number rhymes.

Films

Mathematics in the Cognitively Oriented Curriculum

[EE219] Set of nine color filmstrips and cassette tapes; 163 min total

A series of programs dealing with the mathematical reasoning abilities of children during different stages of intellectual development. The presentations use scenes of the classroom and teacher-planning sessions to show that children's math experience can and should be integrated with their everyday activities. They demonstrate how teachers can use various child-initiated situations to help children think mathematically and use mathematics to solve problems they encounter in their work. The three parts of each filmstrip set deal with the preoperational child, the "transitional" child, and the concrete operational child, respectively.

Understanding and Using the Concept of Number
[EE220] (56 min)

Understanding and Using the Concept of Length
[EE221] (56 min)

Understanding and Using the Concepts of Area, Volume, and Weight
[EE222] (51 min)

Write or call the High/Scope Foundation, 600 North River Street, Ypsilanti, MI 48197, (313) 485-2000 to obtain information on ordering these materials.

11/Spatial relations

Spatial relations—how things take up space, move, and relate to other things in space—occur everywhere in the physical world. Preschoolers explore the ways things relate to one another in space—how things look and feel; what kinds of edges, shapes, and contours things have; how things fit together; how things can be transformed from one shape to another and changed from one position or point of view to another; where things are located; how three-dimensional things look in two dimensions, drawn on a piece of paper. Experiencing and representing spatial relations are essential ingredients in the life of any preschooler, as well as the cornerstones of future scientific and problem-solving abilities.

1. Developing concepts of spatial relations

Review pages 238-40 in **Young Children in Action.** Then answer the following questions:

a) Skye, a five-month-old, is playing with a wooden train car, but when it disappears under the couch, she picks up a rubber cow to play with. Her three-year-old sister Jessie, however, retrieves the train car and gives it back to Skye who is delighted by its reappearance. What does Jessie understand about spatial relations that Skye doesn't, and why is their understanding different?

b) Imagine that you are a one-month-old infant lying on your back on the living room floor. Your parents and three-year-old brother are working and playing nearby.

  1. What objects might pass through your field of vision?

  2. Would any of these objects seem related or connected to anything else? Why or why not?

  3. Your brother is holding a rattle up for you to look at. In the space below, draw what you might see.

  4. Your three-year-old brother starts a game of rattle peek-a-boo. What does he understand about spatial relations that enables him to play this game?

237

c) Describe any memories you have of how things or people looked to you as a very young child.

d) How do barriers influence preschoolers' judgments of proximity and separation?

e) Adults call upon their highly developed spatial understanding every day. Describe the spatial understanding you would have to exercise to complete each of the following tasks:

1. You are a police artist. A group of witnesses are describing a suspect and you are drawing a composite portrait.

2. Your neighbor has recently been confined to a wheelchair. You and a group of other neighbors are designing and building a ramp for his front porch.

3. A friend of yours has moved to an upstairs apartment. The only way she can get her piano up is via the exterior fire-escape stairs. You agree to help her.

4. You have bought your little sister a pedal tractor for her birthday. Now, with instructions and pictures in one hand and a box full of parts in the other, you begin to assemble it.

5. Your aunt, uncle, and two teenaged cousins are coming to visit you at your current residence. You are figuring out where they are all going to sleep.

f) Describe a spatial problem you have recently solved.

2. Recognizing spatial key experiences

Spatial learning occurs wherever preschoolers and objects get together. To recognize these occurrences, review the spatial key experiences listed below:

Key Experiences: Spatial Relations

- Fitting things together and taking them apart

- Rearranging and reshaping objects

- Observing and describing things from different spatial viewpoints

- Experiencing and describing the relative positions, directions, and distances of things

- Experiencing and representing one's own body

- Learning to locate things in the classroom, school, and neighborhood

- Interpreting representations of spatial relations in drawings, pictures, and photographs

- Distinguishing and describing shapes

---

a) Turn to the photographs indicated in **Young Children in Action.** Briefly describe each photograph and list the spatial key experience(s) depicted.

Page	Brief Description	Spatial Key Experience(s)
34		
43 (right)		
52 (all three)		
61		
64-65 (entire sequence)		

Page	Brief Description	Spatial Key Experience(s)
66 (bottom)		
77		
95 (top)		
135 (both)		
141		
149		
174		
182		
199		
204		
225		
234		
241 (top)		

Page	Brief Description	Spatial Key Experience(s)
241 (bottom)		
249		
252		
263		
266		

b) Review and discuss exercise *a* with your team members.

3. Room arrangement and spatial learning

A well-arranged preschool classroom promotes spatial learning. Do the following exercises with your teaching team.

a) A well-arranged classroom enables children to locate the things they need within it. Describe the role of each of the following features in helping children *learn to locate things in their classroom:*

1. Well-defined work areas

2. Consistency

3. Classification of materials

b) How can a well-arranged classroom help children *observe and describe things from different spatial viewpoints?*

c) For circle time, you and your teaching team are planning to focus on *experiencing and describing the relative positions, directions, and distances of things.* You decide to play "Simon Says" and use the whole classroom in the game. How would you play this game? (In your description, include at least ten things Simon would say.)

d) How could you use a well-arranged classroom to help children *interpret representations of spatial relations in drawings, pictures, and photographs?*

e) You and your teaching team have decided to rearrange the classroom to accommodate a music area. How could you involve the children and make this into an experience in *rearranging and reshaping objects?*

4. Spatial learning: Active learning

Spatial learning is active learning. Many adults try to turn spatial learning into a series of directions for children to follow: "Put your hand *on* your head." "Put the pencils *into* the pencil box." "Paste the *round* piece *next to* the *square* piece." One way adults can avoid just giving directions is to set up spatial problems for children to solve that encourage children to act and then to describe their acts in words. For example,

"Where else can you put your hand, Elmen?"

"Here."

"Where's here?"

"In my pocket."

For each of the following situations, you will identify the spatial key experience(s) being emphasized. Then, wherever you find direction-giving and verbal drill, you will describe ways to include action and problem solving.

a) It's small-group time. Mrs. Gridpipe-Fin has given each child a set of nuts and bolts. "Now, when I say, 'Go!' you twist the nuts onto the bolts. Ready? Go!" The children get busy fitting and twisting. "Stop!" calls Mrs. Gridpipe-Fin. "Oh, that's very nice, Eleanor. You twisted all your nuts up to the very top of your bolts. And, Timothy, you twisted yours to the middle. Oh dear, Milo, you just got yours started. You get busy and twist those nuts up from the bottom all the way to the top. . . Good! Now, this time when I say, 'Go!' everybody twist his nuts down, down, down, and off so they're all apart again. Ready? Go!"

1. Identify the spatial key experience(s).

2. Describe ways to include spatial problem solving.

b) "Look at my snake, Teacher," Logan calls from the art area.

"My," responds Mr. Cringingnut, "that's a long one, all right. But I'd like a basket. Let me see you change that snake into a basket. Curl him right around himself into a basket."

1. Identify the spatial key experience(s).

244

2. Describe ways to include spatial problem solving.

c) "Anthony, you're way on top of the climber. I bet things look really different up there." Mrs. Bannister is talking to Anthony at outside time. "How about if you hang upside down so your hands and head dangle down. . . Good! Now I bet I look upside down to you. You sure look upside down to me!"

1. Identify the spatial key experience(s).

2. Describe ways to include spatial problem solving.

d) "Look, Teacher, I put all the pinecones away."

"Good, Jethro, you put all the pinecones into the canister next to the pot holders? Good. And the plates go under the cups. That's right. Now, if you put the blanket over the dolls, the whole house area will be cleaned up!"

1. Identify the spatial key experience(s).

2. Describe ways to include spatial problem solving.

e) "Okay, today for circle time we're going to have a circle parade doing all kinds of different things with our bodies. I'm going to put a record on and we'll all start out by marching as tall as we can." The music starts and everyone marches around in a circle, being very tall. "Okay, now make your bodies as small as you can make them, just like I'm doing. . ."

1. Identify the spatial key experience(s).

2. Describe ways to include spatial problem solving.

f) Mrs. Follini is reading *Caps for Sale* to the children in her small-group time. "Who can find the monkeys on the top of the tree? Good, Leslee. Now, who can find the flower in front of the house? Very good Maggie. Bob, where's the tree that's farthest away from the peddler? That's right. Michelle, where's the monkey who's looking toward the sky? Great. That's right."

1. Identify the spatial key experience(s).

2. Describe ways to include spatial problem solving.

g) Mrs. Yamaha is playing a shape-sorting game with some children in the quiet area. All the wooden shapes are in a pile and each child has a shape-sorting card. "Everyone get a square to put on your card," Mrs. Yamaha directs. "Good, now everybody get a triangle for your card. That's right. Now, get a square."

1. Identify the spatial key experience(s).

2. Describe ways to include spatial problem solving.

h) Review and discuss exercises *a-g* with your teaching team.

5. Spatial learning: The need for active adults

a) Active learners need active teachers. To see what active teachers do, examine the photographs of learners and teachers from **Young Children in Action** indicated below and fill in the following chart:

Page	What Children Are Doing	What Teachers Are Doing
238		
240		
241 (bottom)		
243		
249		
255		
260		
263		
264		

b) What can you conclude about the teachers in the photographs? How would you describe their roles?

c) Without using words, what are these teachers "saying" about *experiencing and representing one's own body?*

d) Review and discuss exercises *a-c* with your team members.

6. Using spatial key experiences to deal with classroom situations

Everyday classroom situations arise that teaching teams feel they must talk about and plan ways to deal with, should similar situations arise again. The key experiences help teaching teams generate strategies to try.

Together with your team members, read through the following classroom situations. Use the spatial key experiences as a guide for generating the strategies to try for each situation.

a) Mike has been climbing onto and jumping off a large, wooden block in the block area all work time. You want to extend Mike's activity to include more spatial experiences. Using the block-area materials available—blocks, large Tinkertoys, cardboard boxes, small rug-sample pieces—what are two strategies you might plan?

b) Lynnette has been zooming her truck back and forth across the block area, often running into other children's structures. How could you and your team plan to help Lynnette structure and extend her activity? Generate at least two spatial strategies.

c) For a number of days, Marketta has randomly pounded nails into a large piece of wood. What two strategies might you plan to try to make Marketta's pounding a more spatial experience?

d) Troy has spent the first couple of months in preschool doing the same thing, no matter what area of the room he works in—filling and emptying containers. Rather than trying to get him to do something altogether new, you and your teaching team want to help Troy vary this activity by adding some spatial elements to it. What two strategies might you plan?

e) Sam has been trying to fit a small pair of pants onto a large doll. Describe two strategies to help him deal with this spatial problem.

f) Elise's mother is very concerned about the test Elise must take before she enters kindergarten. She is particularly concerned about the shape identification part of the test. In order to allay her fears, plan two active, problem-solving ways to help Elise distinguish and describe shapes.

g) Even though it is midway through the school year, children still depend on you to locate classroom materials for them. Describe two ways you can help children learn to locate classroom materials on their own.

h) You notice that your two student teachers are not interacting with children during outside time. The children usually climb on the climber, swing, throw balls, push each other in the wagons, and just run. What two strategies can you suggest to your two student teachers to involve them with children in outdoor learning?

i) Raymond and Timmy built a large house with the counting cubes in the quiet area. They were so proud of themselves that you let them leave it up until tomorrow. Now you and your team members are discussing other ways you could help the boys "save" their building. You've decided to have them draw a picture of it but are aware that they will need help. Describe two strategies to help them solve this problem of spatial representation.

7. Child study: Spatial relations

Child's Name: _____   Date: _____

Child's Age: _____   Location: _____

- Together with your "child-study" child, plan and set up an obstacle course.

- Take turns going through the course and decide how to change it to make it more exciting or challenging.

- Provide _____ with markers and paper and ask _____ to draw a picture of the course.

- Have _____ dictate a story to go with the picture. Then read it back to _____.

- What did you find out about _____'s concept of space?

8. Observing spatial relations in a preschool classroom

a) Spend a morning in a preschool classroom. As you watch, check off all the items you can in the spatial relations checklist on pages 311-13 in **Young Children in Action.**

b) What are the strengths of this classroom regarding spatial relations?

c) If this were your classroom, what changes would you make to provide more opportunities for spatial learning?

9. Spatial relations issues to ponder

a) Suppose there were a culture in which children were carried continuously by their parents and siblings from birth to age three. How might this physical restriction affect the children's understanding of spatial relations?

b) You have a child in your preschool classroom who is "accident prone," that is, he is so physically active that he is always bumping into things and falling. You have another child who is so cautious that he barely moves. How would you work with these children?

c) What is the relationship between spatial learning and action? And reading?

d) One of the children in your preschool classroom is confined to a wheelchair. How would you provide him with spatial key experiences?

e) How is the ability to look at things from different spatial viewpoints related to the ability to recognize other intellectual and emotional viewpoints?

10. Spatial relation projects

a) Visit three parks or playgrounds and evaluate the opportunities they provide for spatial learning. Design a play area where spatial opportunities abound.

b) Design a fit-together-take-apart toy or game using things found in a hardware store. If you can't afford to make what you design, sketch and describe it.

c) Pick out one of your "child-study" child's favorite places or things. Photograph this place or thing from as many different angles and points of view as you possibly can. Show the photographs to the child and record the child's comments and observations. You may want to make a book together.

d) Go on a shape walk with your "child-study" child. Find all the shapes you can and record what they are and where you saw them. If you photograph your findings, you can end up with another book.

Films

Spatial Learning in the Preschool Years
[PS143) 16 mm film; black & white, sound; 22 min
A view of the preoperational child's understanding of the way things relate to one another in three-dimensional space—the look and feel of objects, their shapes, contours, and edges and the way some things fit next to or inside of one another. This film shows children gaining spatial understanding through exploration and manipulation of objects. Scenes from the High/Scope Preschool suggest ways of providing appropriate classroom materials and experiences for spatial problem solving. There are also scenes showing the development of spatial understanding in infancy.

The Block Area
[PS191] Set of five color filmstrips and cassette tapes; 38.7 min total

3. A Place to Build All Kinds of Structures
(9 min)
How children build up, out, around—shows examples of typical structures and suggests strategies a teacher can use to encourage purposeful building.

Cognitive Development Series
16mm films, color, sound
Each film in this series deals with a different kind of thinking process—classifying, seriating, temporal thinking, spatial understanding—and shows a sequence of curriculum goals and corresponding key experiences for elementary-aged students. Each goal and experience is described briefly and illustrated with classroom examples.

3. Spatial Relations—A Sequence of Exercises
[EE213] (20 min)
Children orient themselves and objects in space and mentally organize their experience of the physical world.

Write or call the High/Scope Foundation, 600 North River Street, Ypsilanti, MI 48197, (313) 485-2000 to obtain information on ordering these materials.

12/Time

Preschoolers do not view time the same way adults do. Basically, they are concerned with present time, with now. They are, however, beginning to view time as a continuum, to understand that things existed before now and things will exist after now. As preschoolers talk about time, describe past events, and anticipate future events in words, they strengthen their ability to understand and deal with the continuity of time. They are beginning to think about a sequential order for past events and to learn the words adults use to represent time. They still have a way to go, however, before their understanding of time begins to resemble that of an adult.

1. Understanding a preschooler's concept of time

Review pages 267-68 in **Young Children in Action,** then answer the following questions:

a) Infants have a one-dimensional concept of time. What does that mean?

b) Preschoolers are just beginning to view time as a continuum. What does that mean?

c) Preschoolers see time subjectively, while adults view time objectively. What is the difference?

d) The word "time" has many meanings in adult conversation. While adults understand the meaning of time in all its various usages, preschoolers are very literal in their understanding. Choose five of the following sentences and describe how a preschooler might interpret them:

He made it to the big time!

Check the timetable to see when Grandma's train comes in.

What's your favorite pastime?

Right now he's just marking time.

If he really wants to do it, he'll make time.

He spends very little time at home.

Time flies when you're having fun.

Time stood still.

I've told you time and time again.

e) Even though preschoolers don't understand the above expressions the way adults do and don't understand what a "minute" or a "year" is, why is it important for adults to use time units and expressions in their everyday conversations with children?

f) How did you perceive time as a young child?

g) Review and discuss exercises *a-f* with your team members.

2. Recognizing time key experiences

Time key experiences fall into two categories: (A) understanding time units or intervals and (B) sequencing events in time.

Key Experiences: Time

A. Understanding time units or intervals

- Stopping and starting an action or signal

- Experiencing and describing different rates of speed

- Experiencing and comparing time intervals

- Observing seasonal changes

- Observing that clocks and calendars are used to mark the passage of time

B. Sequencing events in time

- Anticipating future events verbally and making appropriate preparations

- Planning and completing what one has planned

- Describing and representing past events

- Using conventional time units in talking about past and future events

- Noticing and describing the order of events

Look at the photographs or illustrations on the pages of **Young Children in Action** listed below. Briefly describe each one and list the time key experience(s) illustrated.

Page	Brief Description	Time Key Experience(s)
48		
61		
64 (left)		
65 (right)		
174 (bottom)		
184		
243		
266		
268		
271		
273 (all)		

Page	Brief Description	Time Key Experience(s)
276		
277		
279 (all)		

3. Helping preschoolers understand time limits or intervals

Review pages 268-77 in **Young Children in Action.** Then do the following exercises:

a) Why do preschoolers believe that simultaneous events of the same duration take up different amounts of time? What influences their judgment?

b) Throughout the morning, Sam continually asks, "Is it outside time yet?" Once it finally is outside time, he asks, "Do we have to go in yet?" How could you help him deal more effectively with the beginning and end of this time period that seems to be so important to him?

c) What confusions do preschoolers have about comparing rates of speed?

d) You've decided to concentrate on the time key experience *experiencing and describing different rates of speed* at small-group time.

   1. What materials will you provide for each child?

   2. What will you say to get the small-group time activity started?

   3. What are four things you might expect to see children doing?

   4. What will your role be?

   5. How will you draw the small-group time to a meaningful end?

e) Briefly describe ten different ways children could experience and describe different rates of speed with their own bodies at outside time.

f) Do preschoolers have a sense of a uniform rate of time? Why or why not?

g) Answer the following children's "how-long-until" questions, using time intervals the children can understand.

   1. "When's my mom gonna pick me up?" Denise asks at the beginning of work time.

   2. "Here's some cookies for everybody, Teacher! Can we eat 'em now?" Michelle asks as she arrives at school.
      "No, but we sure can eat them at snack time," you reply.
      "How long's that?" Michelle wants to know.

   3. "When's it going to be my turn on the swing, Teacher?" Jamison asks at outside time.

h) Are preschoolers able to understand the notion of recurrence, time as a cyclical progression? Why or why not?

i) You are visiting a preschool in Miami, Florida. It's January and the teacher is "doing a unit on winter." She has decorated a bulletin board with snowflakes and snowmen cutouts and for circle time she's reading a story about Eskimo children. If this were your classroom in Florida, what changes in the "winter unit" would you make?

j) Why are conventional clocks and calendars beyond the comprehension of preschoolers?

k) A friend of yours is an engineering student who has promised to build you a clock that would make sense to preschoolers. Together, you've decided that it will be a 2½-hour clock and will tell the daily routine time without using numbers or words. What would the face of this clock look like? Draw a picture.

l) Review and discuss exercises *a-k* with your team members.

4. Helping preschoolers sequence events in time

Pages 278-82 in **Young Children in Action** will be of assistance in answering the following questions:

a) Some people live almost completely in the past. Some live in the future, and some live in the here and now, in the present. Where do preschoolers live in time? Why?

b) What do preschoolers gain as they begin to anticipate future events?

c) What do preschoolers gain as they begin to recall past events?

d) Which would be easier for preschoolers to do—describe the sequence of the seasons or describe the sequence of steps involved in putting together the airplanes they just made? Why?

e) Marketta comes bursting into school after a few days absence with this story: "Tomorrow my dog got hit by the car. We were so sad so my dad says we're going to get a new dog yesterday when she gets borned from her mother. I'm going to have my new dog today when she gets her eyes open. When she drinks milk from her mother she has to stay with her mother till she gets big." How would you respond to this story both acknowledging Marketta's enthusiasm and her attempt to sequence events in time?

f) Review and discuss exercises *a-e* with your team members.

5. Using time to deal with everyday situations

Solve the following problems with your team members:

a) At outside time, Timmy, Lynnette, Corey, and Sam are arguing about whose turn it is to steer the ride-on taxi. How can you help them solve this problem, using one of the time key experiences as a guide?

b) Clarice is walking on the balance beam but keeps bumping into Brenda who is in front of her. How can you help her solve this problem, using one of the time key experiences as a guide?

c) Troy has planned to make fingerpaint and use it as he did yesterday, but before you can get to him, he dumps some orange tempra powder on the table and is swishing it around with his hands. How can you retrieve the situation by looking at it as an opportunity to work with Troy on time?

d) Raymond, Michelle, and Mike planned to work in the music area. They started out trying different instruments, but now they are all banging on at least two instruments apiece, growing louder and louder. How can you join them and redirect their concertizing to focus on one or two of the time key experiences?

e) Denise is anxious to have her father pick her up at the end of school, so after she takes off her coat, she goes to the window to wait for him. How can you help her gain a sense of when he will be returning?

6. Child study: Time

Child's Name: _____   **Date:** _____

Child's Age: _____   **Location:** _____

- Together with _____, make up a stopping and starting game. Play it.

- Together with _____, set up a race. (You might decide to race two cars down a ramp made from a block, for example). Ask _____ thought-provoking questions about different rates of speed and time intervals. Ask _____ to predict who is going to win each race and why.

- After you have done the previous exercises together, ask _____ to draw a picture and tell a story about what you have done together.

- What did you learn about the child's concept of time?

7. Observing time key experiences in a preschool classroom

Visit a preschool classroom and check off the items that apply in the time checklist on pages 313-14 of **Young Children in Action.**

a) What are the strengths of this classroom regarding time?

b) If this were your preschool classroom, what changes would you make to provide more time key experiences for children?

8. Time issues to ponder

a) Suppose that you are about to have a baby and a clock supplier offers to furnish you with clocks. You have to choose between regular face clocks, or digital clocks, or a mixture of both. Which would you choose, realizing that as your baby grows he or she is going to learn about telling time from these clocks. Explain your choice.

b) What kind of atmosphere would you try to create in your preschool classroom: one in which children are hurried along to the next thing, one in which children have all the time in the world they need, or one somewhere in the middle? Explain your choice.

c) Do you have to set aside time to teach preschoolers about time? Why or why not?

d) Do preschool children from different cultures have different notions of time? Why or why not?

e) How would you acquaint a blind preschooler with clocks and calendars?

f) How does a daily routine help preschoolers understand time concepts?

g) What is the relationship between time and number? Between time and seriation?

9. Time projects

a) Design a personal clock or calendar for your "child-study" child. If your first effort is confusing to _____, make necessary modifications.

b) During a 24-hour period, make a note of all the references to time you see or hear. How would a preschooler interpret each one?

c) Find a group of children in second or third grade who are learning to tell time. What do they understand about clock time? What is confusing for them? For children to tell time, what are all the concepts they have to understand? List them.

d) Ask your "child-study" child to explain these statements to you. Record his or her answers.

A stitch in time saves nine.

Time flies when you're having fun.

Time marches on.

Time and tide wait for no man.

How old do you think a child has to be to understand the statements? Test out your hypothesis on several older children.

e) Design and try out a movement activity that would provide preschoolers with one or more time key experiences.

Films

Learning About Time in the Preschool Years
[PS141] 16mm film; black & white, sound; 37.5 min
This film shows how teachers can help children understand concepts of time; it illustrates strategies for encouraging children to recall the past, anticipate the future, and observe and represent temporal sequences and intervals. The first part shows how to help children observe the beginning and end of time periods, observe movement and change, and begin to represent the passage of time. The second part shows how young children learn to anticipate and recall events and observe and predict the order in which events occur.

Cognitive Development Series
16mm films, color, sound
Each film in this series deals with a different kind of thinking process—classifying, seriating, temporal thinking, spatial understanding—and shows a sequence of curriculum goals and corresponding key experiences for elementary-aged students. Each goal and experience is described briefly and illustrated with classroom examples.

4. Temporal Relations—A Sequence of Exercises
(on 2 reels) [EE214] (35 min) [EE215] (16 min)
Aspects of the development of the child's orientation in time—ways children learn to understand and function within time.

Write or call the High/Scope Foundation, 600 North River Street, Ypsilanti, MI 48197, (313) 485-2000 to obtain information on ordering these materials.

13/What next?

You have completed the exercises in this book about room arrangement, daily routine, teaching and planning in a team, active learning, language, experiencing and representing, classification, seriation, number, space, and time. Now you must put what you have learned together. The exercises in this chapter will help you think about the next steps you can take toward providing high quality preschool education for young children.

1. Understanding young children

The Cognitively Oriented Curriculum is a way of observing, understanding, and planning for young children.

a) Review all your child-study exercises and write a brief but thorough report of what you know about your "child-study" child. Review the report with the child's parent(s) and/or teacher(s).

b) What things did you find out about your "child-study" child other than the specific things you were observing for? Why?

c) Is there something missing from your report? Something you feel you should know about but don't? What? Why? How would you add this element to your knowledge about your child-study child?

2. Comparing this preschool curriculum to others

Preschool curricula come in many different packages. The key is finding the curriculum that, to your way of thinking, best serves children and their teachers.

a) List the other kinds of preschool curricula with which you are familiar (for example, directed learning, free play, unit-based). What characterizes each of these approaches to learning? What is the role of the child? Of the adults?

b) What does "cognitively oriented" mean?

c) How is the Cognitively Oriented Curriculum similar to these approaches? How is it different?

d) How does the Cognitively Oriented Curriculum encourage children to express their feelings, think about others, and feel good about themselves?

3. Working with a teaching team

The Cognitively Oriented Curriculum depends on team work, daily evaluation and planning, and mutual problem solving.

a) List the strengths and weaknesses of your teaching team.

b) What did you learn about yourself as a group member and a group leader?

c) Interview members of an actual preschool teaching team. What do they see as the problems and satisfactions of teamwork?

d) Where do the members of a teaching team turn when they cannot solve a problem together?

e) Would you be willing to commit yourself to the team-teaching approach? Why or why not?

4. Early childhood issues

a) What are the major issues facing early childhood educators today?

b) How would you deal with these issues?

c)   What do you plan to do next to provide high quality preschool education for young children?

5. Study guide evaluation

a) If it were your job to revise this study guide, what changes would you make?

b) Please share your ideas with us. Send your revisions, suggestions, and comments to:

Study Guide Evaluation
c/o Mary Hohmann
High/Scope Press
600 North River Street
Ypsilanti, MI 48197

Thank you and best wishes in your career in early childhood education.